What Rocks Your World?

Putting Your Talent To Work

Jenny Mullins

CONTENTS

ACKNOWLEDGEMENTS

It is said that everyone has a book inside them and I was aware over the last few years that I had something I wanted to share. Not a list of do's and don'ts but rather a friendly voice offering reassurance, encouragement and top tips along the way. As a Careers Adviser I have often wanted to refer young people to a good book that offered support rather than masses of information. When I couldn't find such a book for teenagers in the UK, I set myself a challenge to write it.

From watching the talent shows on TV, I could see the similarity between the process of dreaming about success to it actually happening. This book is me being your mentor and supporting you all the way. Let me know how you get on; tweet or email me. It will be great to share your journey.

I must thank my supporters too: those who have read through my endless drafts and suggestions.

Starting with the teenagers I wrote this for, thanks to Abby, Lucy and Perry.

The eagle eyed proof readers Paul and Rish.

My careers 'birds' - Alex, Rach, Maria, Sophie, Jayne, Dashi, Lucy and Fiona.

The 'Drs' - Chris Jones, Gezim Alpion, Jayne Sayers and Jubayer Ahmed for their additional input.

Special thanks to Nigel and Matt for their wealth of suggestions, encouragement, revisions and corrections: all duly taken on board.

A special thanks to 'everyone needs a Ruth' Lawton and Eluned Jones for giving me opportunities in Higher Education careers work.

To my family and friends for rocking my world.

Most importantly this book would be nowhere without my husband, Nick. Literally, in that he painstakingly edited it, patiently corrected my spelling and formatted it to this book you are reading today. But more than that, he provided me with endless cups of tea and hugs of encouragement. We all need a team of supporters and I feel very blessed to have mine.

This book is dedicated to Nick, my Grandad Harry Ward and all the young people that I have had the privilege of meeting over the years.

INTRODUCTION

Did you dread the question that all relatives ask at some point?

"So, what are you going to be when you grow up?"

Personally, I hated it. I felt as though I had to give an answer that showed that I had already thought about it - a definite idea that met with everyone's approval. The truth was that I really didn't have a definite idea at all. I didn't want to say just anything. But the scary fact was that I couldn't really describe what I wanted to be.

However, I was very sure about what I didn't want to do. I wasn't very good at science and I wasn't interested in building or making things. In fact, I knew I wasn't a 'things' person at all. I knew that I liked people, but that was way too vague. I didn't want to be a doctor or a nurse, and I didn't think I wanted to be a teacher. Beyond that I just wasn't sure. I enjoyed English, History, RE, researching and writing - just getting under the skin of people. Could I have a job where I got to help people, talk to them, try to understand them and encourage them too?

I was 22 years old before I started to wrestle with where I was going next and began to take some steps forward. I certainly didn't know what I wanted to be when I was choosing my options in year nine... or when I chose my work experience or even when I applied to University. But looking back, I had made some good choices along the way... or did they choose me?

Over the last 20 years, I have worked as a Careers Adviser and Youth Worker and had the privilege of meeting many incredible young people. Their questions have ranged from very specific things, such as:

"How do I get to be a nurse?"

Through to more unusual questions like:

"What training do I need to breed guinea pigs?"

Some people had very specific ideas... others knew that they wanted to do something... others worried because they had absolutely no ideas. What they all had in common was that they were on a journey of discovery. Destination unknown for some: destination clearer for others.

Here's some reassurance. This book isn't about setting out your career path for you and it certainly isn't about telling you what you should be or what job you should take. But it is about encouraging you to generate your own ideas.

Look around. Get on the internet. Talk to people. Keep your options open. Believe that there are many things that you can potentially do. Take the pressure off yourself to give an exact title to what you want to do. If you do know, then that's great - but there are many other related ideas that you might want to explore.

I have seen people with no ideas, desperate to discover what they want to do next and they beat themselves up about it. Those that have ideas worry about what happens if they don't get on to that course or into that career area. Also there is that frequent concern of 'what happens if I get there and I don't actually like what I do?'

This book will explore the various options that are open to you and guide you through the process. Are you ready to find out what rocks your world?

- Good starting point. It's the bit behind the scenes. Maybe you have never told anyone before.
- Find out the things that you enjoy doing, what you are good at as well as what is important to you.
- It doesn't assume you will have lots of careers ideas, but that you probably have an idea about what you like, what is important to you, what makes you tick?
- **What rocks your world?**

- The audition stage is about enquiring and researching.
- Find out the secret of people's success.
- Get a group of supporters around you and sound out your ideas with them.
- What do they know about you? What advice do they have for you as you try out your ideas?

- What is the competition and how can you stand out from the crowd?
- Get involved, focus on action and put your talent to work.
- Establish a support network with mentors/coaches to help achieve your goals.
- Have showcase finals in sight and book your place.

- This is the time to let the hard work pay off and let your talent shine.
- Show that you have done your research and can demonstrate how you stand out from the crowd.
- Perform under the spotlight and discover what is on the checklist of the 'judges'.
- Prove your own style and experience is just what the judges are looking for.
- Put your talent to work.

Jenny Mullins

JUST ME

Let's start by looking at ways in which you can find out the things that you enjoy doing - what you are good at as well as what's important to you. What rocks your world now can really help when it comes to exploring career ideas.

Go on, tell me about yourself and just start with one thing. Tell me more. Imagine you are writing your life story. You are the main character and I want you to set the scene for me. How old are you? Where were you born? Where do you live now and who do you live with? What do you look like? More importantly, who would you like to play yourself in the big blockbuster film about your life? I've always had Cameron Diaz in mind to play me... but that's another story.

Giving the details about our lives can actually be fairly straight forward (although if you did get hold of a picture, you might not see that much of resemblance between me and Cameron Diaz). Check out the photo of me on the What Rocks Your World website (www.whatrocksyourworld.com) and see if you can spot a resemblance!

But hold on. This isn't a book about my life story. It's about yours. Go back to my first question. Tell me about yourself. The stuff that you are not sure about. The things that make you **you**. This is about who you are and where you would like to be. What you would like to do in life. It's about **your** dreams, **your** passions and the things that make **you** tick.

I have interviewed thousands of young people over the years and I'm constantly surprised and amazed by the ideas you have. What you do in your spare time and what rocks your world. What motivates you and the reason that you can't wait for the weekends.

Even the identical twins I interviewed had different ideas about what they would like to do (although interviewing them on the same day was confusing). You are unique - and because you are unique it means that you will have different ideas about what you want to do. Plus, I suspect some of you don't have any ideas about what you want to do. It really is okay to not know. Not having a plan at this stage is completely fine. Because this book is written to help you work out what you would like to do and then put that into action.

I've used the reality-talent-show format to help understand the process that you will go through in making decisions about the future. Think of applying for any opportunity as being part of a talent show.

So this section is about the step that you don't see on the reality shows. It's the part behind the scenes - it's the singing into the hair brush when we think no-one is listening. It's lying on our beds wondering what life is about and what we might be doing in the future. The cameras will never go here. Allow yourself to dream 'What if...'

Behind the scenes

Some people seem to know from a very early age what they would like to do when they are older. I have interviewed adults who have been in their job for many years and will say that they knew what they wanted to do from the age of seven. On the other hand, I have also met many people who said that when they grew up they would like to do a number of things, only to end up doing something completely different.

Having ideas is great. What is helpful is to start to think about what you would like out of a job and out of your life. Your job may decide how you live your day-to-day life.

A pilot will need to plan ahead and will have their life determined by shifts, time zones and resting periods. A vet knows that they may be called out in the middle of the night to a cow struggling to give birth. A soldier may have their holiday cancelled if there is a national emergency. Teachers will have to do parent events and paramedics may not clock-off in time to put the children to bed. Some people are quite happy to have stable hours and know that each day is likely to be similar. Others would find that dull. Do you want to travel? Would you like to go to the same place every day?

Just as we all have a different favourite flavour of ice cream, we are all very different.

Let's start with what you enjoy doing

It doesn't have to be a school subject - although if it is something that you learn, that's fine. What do you enjoy doing? Describe it to me. Imagine I don't know what that activity is. Talk me through what you **do**, what you **think** and what you **feel** when you are engaged in this activity.

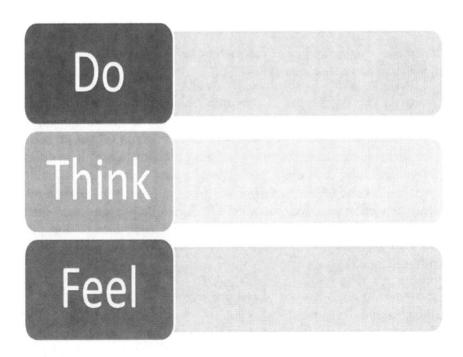

If you want to download and print off any of the worksheets in this book then go to www.whatrocksyourworld.com and look at the 'VIP Access' section. To make the most of this book you will find worksheets for activities on the website. You will need a password and this can be found at the start of **The Audition Stage**. You can do the worksheets if you want to, or else just keep reading. Do whatever helps you.

Can you think of a job or activity that would allow you to do something that you enjoy?

Think big!

There are thousands of job roles out there (if you don't believe me, as a good starting point check out these two websites). You could even research the word 'jobs' and see what comes up.

www.careercamel.com

www.nationalcareersservice.direct.gov.uk

There are also a number of careers guides that look at job types and qualifications or training needed.

There are two main types of activities: making things and providing a service. Over the years, jobs have changed. As technology changes, so do the jobs. IT jobs were scarce over 30 years ago. Instead, many people made things in the manufacturing industry. Customer service call centres have shot up, as have the increases in internet marketing, social media and websites. *CSI: Crime Scene Investigation* has shown that crime detection practices focus on DNA sampling and sophisticated forensic activities. During your life time, jobs have changed and they will continue to do so. The job that you end up doing may not even currently exist!

So try not to limit yourself to just one job idea at the moment and be open to the fact that new roles are developing all of the time. Without the aid of time travel, we can't completely predict the future. But what we can do is look at your potential. We have started with just one thing that you enjoy doing. Now think about a strength. Think about something that you do well. These things are also known as skills or talents. It might even be different from something you enjoy doing. For example, I am very good at maths, but can honestly say that I don't enjoy doing it all that much. Let's start by identifying a strength. From here we can find examples that are evidence to prove that strength.

How could that strength be applied? If you are good with computers, you could show that you are good at it when you create spreadsheets, set up databases or word-process documents. You may also use a strength to draw in Design Technology lessons or design flyers for the school's Christmas fair. You could apply those skills to designing posters and creating multimedia presentations.

My
strength is

I am good
at it when

How could
I apply it?

Following on from the example of IT, start to think about the types of jobs that use computers. Software designers and IT technicians clearly use IT. But what about air traffic controllers? Or medical staff? Or graphic designers? In fact, most jobs these days will require you to be good at IT. Looking at the job websites mentioned earlier will help with this.

But choosing a career isn't just about something that you can do. You will have many things that you are good at and later on, I am going to encourage you to find out what you are good at from the people that know you.

Have a go at writing five things that you are good at:

1.

2.

3.

4.

5.

Not bad eh? But how many are linked to school subjects? Now give me another five things that you are good at. This time focus on other things, such as hobbies, sports and activities.

1.

2.

3.

4.

5.

Have a go at ranking them in order, or at least identify your **top three:**

1.

2.

3.

But what about the things that people may not know about you (the stuff you might want to keep to yourself in your diary)? It's the things that you value in life - what really matters to you. We call these areas your values and priorities.

I have come across a number of students who will not work for certain companies because they disapprove of what a company stands for and what it has done in the past. For example, although they know that they could make a lot of money developing missile technology they are uncomfortable that they would be part of an industry that is involved in warfare. Some will want to make as much money as possible. Others would rather help organisations raise money for the community or a particular charity. This might not be a big issue for you, but I have known some people who believe so passionately in something that it frames their entire life.

So far, we've looked at your strengths and what you are good at. We are now going to look at what is important to you and discover if there is something that really rocks your world?

A few questions that you might want to ask yourself are:

What is important to me?

Imagine that you are being interviewed at the start of your career:

What do I hope for?

Fast forward five years:

What would I like to see myself doing?

Where would I be living?

And whilst we are **thinking big…**

> ## What would I like to be my greatest achievement so far?

> ## Who (or what) will have helped me along the way?

> ## What would I like to be remembered for?

Look at all of your life, not just what goes on at school because there are a few questions that you might want to ask yourself. If you do complete this worksheet then take your time and be as honest as you can. The only person looking at your answers is you.

It's all about knowing your own style

Walk through your average town centre and you will see lots of different types - the sporty look, emos and the trend setters. We all like to express ourselves in a certain way. Priorities and values are one way that we can stand out from the crowd. Motivation and passion are other characteristics. Asking two opposing football fans why their team should win the FA Cup Final will bring out a passion for each team. Some people can motivate themselves to get up in all weathers to train for a big sporting event. Others won't move until their alarm screeches at them that they have just 15 minutes to get ready for school.

What would I do all day, if given the choice?

What am I doing when I don't notice the time or I lose myself in an activity?

What do I really love doing?

Which websites do I follow avidly?

If I could have a dream job, it would be.....

The answers to these questions can be a great clue as to what you might want to do in the future. It has been described as being in the 'flow' when you completely lose yourself in an activity and feel content with what you are doing. It could be drawing, running or trying to solve a puzzle. But studies have shown that being in the 'flow' increases satisfaction and happiness at work. So, if you love doing something now, maybe that could be a clue to something you might want as part of your life in the future.

When it comes to getting things done, how likely am I to do them on time?

When it means having to put the effort in, how do I react?

Out of ten, how motivated am I to do my homework?

How is your motivation level after all of these questions?

Hopefully it didn't feel too much like an inquisition or an exam. But the combination of all the right ingredients can be really important to careers choice. Too much passion and not enough motivation may mean that you don't ever really get round to doing it. Having great skills but no enjoyment might lead to frustration. How well do you know yourself?

Because this is the **Just Me** stage the answers are just for you. They are designed to get you thinking about what you might want and how well you know yourself. Maybe in a year's time you will feel differently about things. But it's a good starting point. Once we have got a few things in place, the other pieces should soon follow.

Tweet Challenge: What is the main thing you have learnt about yourself in this chapter? Tweet me @whatrocksyou.

AUDITION STAGE

Want to know what others think about you? Want to find out the secret of others' success and how they got to do different jobs? What rocks their world? And what if your very own supporters had some great tips? It's time to get interviewing those around you...

This stage is about moving on from the privacy of your own space - whether it's singing into the hairbrush or lying on your bed and just wondering what life is about and where you fit in. It requires confidence. But trust me, it will be alright. That's because you've already done the hard bit, which is to ask yourself some really big and private questions. It's like you've written a private diary when you are sure that no-one will get to see it (especially your prying little sister).

Talk and listen

So we've looked at the things that perhaps we only know ourselves. We're now going to audition. What this involves is moving to a point where you can sound your ideas out with someone. It's like moving some of your ideas from a private diary to a blog. When you know what you want to talk about, try to find someone or some people who will be good to talk to. This audition stage isn't meant to be a scary process (even though the talent shows may hype this process up). See this as a sounding out process. During this stage, it's about testing out your thoughts and ideas with a group of people who know you. It's not about harsh criticism. They may be experts in a certain area, but the main thing is that they can give you an honesty check.

So, who might these people be?

Parents, family, friends, teachers, careers advisers, youth workers, activity leaders are all good starting points. When you ask them for an honesty check, the rules are simple – they have to be constructive. This isn't the **Showcase Final**, when you are being judged. This part is about asking for ideas and feedback. It shouldn't be about others taking control over your life or overwhelming you. If they start to do that then show them the red card (destructive comment alert) and move on!

This is the exploration stage and people that know you well may be able to see things that you can't. If you need a few pointers for questions, look to the worksheets. Let them know that you are enthusiastic to find out as much about yourself as possible.

Questions to ask others about what they know about ME...

Talent
- What are my talents/strengths?
- What am I good at/not so good at?

Skills
- Which are my best subjects at school?
- What do I do best?

Passion
- What am I passionate about?
- What three words describe me?

Motivation
- How motivated am I?
- How likely am I to get things done?

To do list
- Which specific parts of my life do I need to work on?
- How can I improve on these areas?

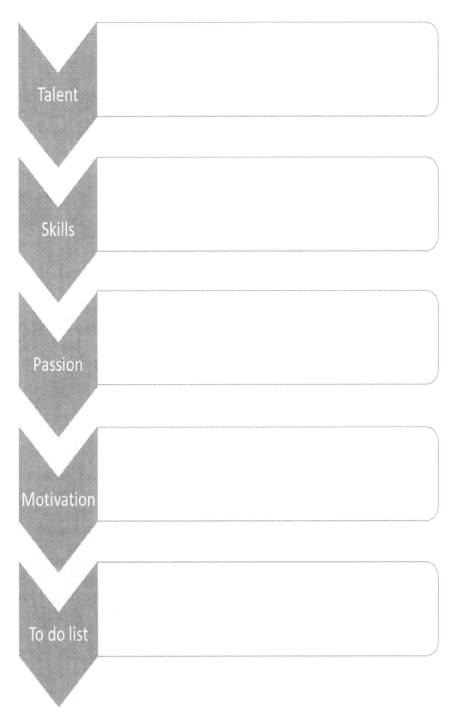

How does this match up to what you thought about yourself?

Any surprises? Do you have things to work on? Notice the to-do list. Others will often have suggestions from their own experiences that can help you identify areas to work on, or things to follow up. Asking as many people as possible from different areas of your life will help you to get a full picture.

The password for all the worksheets on the website is 'wrywstar'.

Next step: to find out about other people and their jobs

It's your turn to be the interviewer. You don't need to stop people in the street, but you might want to start off with your family and people that know you well. A good starting point is to find out what they have done in their lives.

When did **they** know what they wanted to do?

How have they changed over the years?

As the interviewer, tell them that you are just exploring what is out there. What you will find is that if you show interest most people are happy to talk about their roles/jobs. Some will even share with you the 'secrets of their success' and how they made their decisions.

There are some golden rules: always be polite and check if they are happy for you to make notes. Be clear on what questions you would like to ask. There are some suggestions below, but you may have some of your own thoughts and want to get specific about their career path.

In these interviews, listen to what they have to say

A good starting point is to ask people what three bits of advice they would give to you and what would they say if they had to write a letter to their teenage self?

The world might be changing, but be inquisitive and go and enquire. Other good questions to ask are:

How did you find your job(s)?

How did you end up in your current situation?

How much was planned?

How much was luck/chance/just happened?

If they are happy to talk, find out what they wanted to do at certain ages.

You might well be surprised at the plans and the reality! Can you see a pattern at all? When your parents or grandparents were looking at their futures, there was often an emphasis on planning and sticking with a set route and to keep climbing a career ladder. More recently, the last generation have seen much more movement, going from different types of work and interests. There's a good chance you will have lots of different jobs/roles throughout your life.

So, ask your interviewers about what they have done and how their lives have changed.

What was important to you as a teenager?

What was important to you at different times in your life?

Important things are called values and priorities.

Owning and driving a fast car might be a priority at 25, but not at 35, when baby number two is on the way.

Apart from gathering all of this information, what can you apply from their lives to yours?

If they had one piece of advice, what would it be?

Try and talk to people of different ages and backgrounds - the more, the better. If you find it difficult to meet people, ask others if they can recommend people you can interview. If it's through Facebook or email, focus on how you write your request, as first impressions really do count.

If it's the first time someone hears from you, make it a good first impression. Keep it brief. Explain you are thinking about your future but keen to find out what makes people successful and would like one piece of advice that would help you. Be polite and thank them for their time.

You could even use Twitter. By emailing or tweeting to find out more, you might be overwhelmed by some exciting and surprising ideas.

Don't forget to check both spelling and grammar. The biggest complaint that employers make is about these two things. So save your text speak for texts and Facebook.

In all of this, I want to encourage you to be excited

Remember in the story of Aladdin, the genie grants Aladdin three wishes? Imagine that **you** are granted three wishes, but this time they have conditions. This genie says that you can have a party in any place in the world, with whatever food, drink and entertainment you want. But you must choose three people who have inspired you or who you would love to meet.

Who would you choose? Now, while you are thinking, you need to do your research to find out a bit about their lives. What subjects did they take? What was their biggest break? How did they achieve their goals and get successful? I have just looked at three people I would love at my party: Bill Gates, Michelle Obama and Martin Lewis (the money saving expert). Successes in their own ways. Research your party list and jot down what you have discovered. If you email your dream guests and get a personal reply, you are getting that head start.

Having asked people about their journeys and what rocks their world, it's now a good time see what is out there. Apart from careers books, you can go to the websites of organisations in areas ranging from accountancy to zoo keeping, and everything else in between. At this auditioning stage, you might want to keep it as broad as possible. Good websites to start off with are:

www.nationalcareersservice.direct.gov.uk

www.careercamel.com

www.prospects.ac.uk

www.targetjobs.co.uk

www.yourcareerguide.co.uk

If you want meatier detail, look at the professional organisations, or maybe do this at the Boot Camp stage, when you are confident you can get a plan together.

Listen to the feedback and ask yourself what you have learnt

A great visual way to see what the key points are is to type up the answers and to make a Wordle (a pictorial dream cloud) of what they have said.

www.wordle.net

So, what next? It's possible that you've discovered that not everyone's successes were planned and that both setbacks and nice surprises can happen at different times. Don't feel pressured to map everything out at this stage. Sometimes the things which are unplanned can actually turn out to be great opportunities. It doesn't mean you have failed just because you don't get something straight away, in fact you can learn from most things and turn them into positives. And you can use these things as examples of your perseverance when you meet the judges.

Have a go yourself

We've talked about passions, motivations and interests. We've also looked at ways to find things out, by interviewing and listening. The best way is often to try things out. When it comes to certain skill areas, you will be able to try things out in subject lessons in school or college. What better way to learn about written communication skills than by writing assignments and presenting information in a report or project?

But how about your listening skills?

Or working as part of a team?

Solving problems?

Being organised and on time?

School or college can definitely help you develop these skills. But what is it like in the workplace?

Taking advantage of tasters or work shadowing is a great opportunity. We'll be talking about work experience much more in the **Boot Camp** stage. But if you want to try something out, then see if you can give it a go. Take advantage of structured opportunities or look to join clubs or groups that will help you gain experience about an area, as well as find out a bit more for yourself. Volunteering is a great way to learn new skills, gain confidence and make new friends.

Plus, who knows what it could lead on to? Have a look at this website for information about volunteering in your area – www.vinspired.com.

Ready to sound out your thoughts with a group of supporters? It's often so much easier when you have a team of supporters behind you. Even at the audition stage, most people will want friends and family with them.

During this chapter, you've already started to think of people who can give you some great ideas, tips and inspire you to try things out. The next step is to move it forward. The audition stage is about enquiring and researching. Now it's time to get serious, draw up that training plan and get ready for **Boot Camp**.

> **Tweet Challenge: What is the main thing you have learnt about other people's careers in this chapter? Tweet me @whatrocksyou.**

BOOT CAMP

Part 1

Introducing Boot Camp and what it means to be SMART

In this section, we will look at getting support from mentors to help us achieve our goals. What is the competition and how do you stand out from the crowd? Do you want a great CV and covering letter for work experience or a job? Want to know what options there are? How do you impress those judges and get selected for the finals? You might find it helpful to start with the part which introduces **Boot Camp** and getting a mentor first. Then go to the part which covers where you are in your studies.

The phrase 'boot camp' started as a reference to the style of boots worn by the US military, but is now often used to refer to a place for providing basic military training for new soldiers. But with programmes like *'X Factor'* and other reality and fitness programmes, the term is increasingly being used to refer to training hard. It is to do with getting into shape and overcoming obstacles, with sights firmly set on achieving goals. In *'The Voice UK'* it is even pitched as preparing for the battle. **Boot Camp** is hard work, but likely to get some great results. If the **Audition Stage** is about sounding out ideas and doing the behind the scenes work, the **Boot Camp** stage is about action, getting involved and putting your talent to work. It's all about careers fitness. But what is that and how do you get it?

Quite simply, careers fitness is about being prepared to tackle whatever it takes to be successful. It requires commitment and a willingness to give it a go, believing that progress can be made. The success of **Boot Camp** is that it is designed to get you focused, to set some targets in place and work towards them.

It is often said that if you write your goals down then you will achieve them. Most New Year resolutions last for a few weeks and then disappear. How many times have we all promised to eat less chocolate throughout the year and vowed to be healthier, only to have given up within weeks? For many of us, the motivation goes and that general feeling of wanting to do something better has soon disappeared.

One way to be successful is to write down something very specific about what you would like to achieve and to get someone to help you.

"I will get fit by riding my bike more" is too vague.

What does *"more"* mean?

Every day?   One more time than last year?

BUT...

If you write: *"I will ride my bike on Sunday afternoon for 45 minutes every week"*

It is specific - it identifies an activity, time and date.

It is measurable – the activity can be proved and timed.

It is achievable.

There is a realistic chance of reaching a goal.

And it is linked to a definite time.

This is often known as S M A R T.

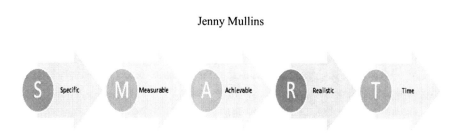

Go back to what you learnt from the **Audition Stage** and reflect on what has worked so far. What have you learnt?

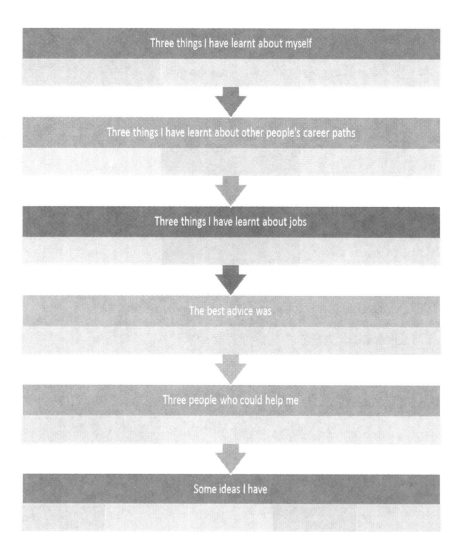

Let's look at your ideas. At this stage, we are looking to find a few things out and get ready to follow ideas through. What you may have learnt is that some people are very good at planning their careers. They made a decision fairly early on, chose the right subjects, got the right experience and training, and ended up in their career. They had a goal in mind and they went for it.

For some, maybe it was almost as if the career found them! They might have been in the right place at the right time. My sister Jo ended up taking her course at University because I noticed in the local newspaper that there were some spaces on a new law degree and Jo was looking for a law course. Chance? Possibly. Being in the right place at the right time? Definitely. Using her network of people around her? Absolutely. Knowing it was a great opportunity? Well, it certainly turned her eye. But she was keen to find out more and see if it was right for her. She knew what she wanted, but she still had to make some enquiries to see if it really was right for her. Jo's lesson: check out the small print and then if you think it's a great opportunity, go for it!

Not everything in life works out according to all the plans we make. This isn't about giving up now and saying *"what's the point?"* Rather, it's about saying, *"I can't control everything in life and I need to be ready for plan B"*. Plus, if you have an enquiring mind and believe that good opportunities can turn up, you need to make sure that you have the right skills and motivation to follow things through. Also, if you have people on your side, looking out for you, who care about your future - you have a huge advantage.

Part 2

Finding the right mentor or coach

'Mentor - an experienced person who advises and helps somebody with less experience over a period of time.'

Oxford Advanced Learner's Dictionary

A mentor could also be described as a trusted individual, friend or teacher. Mentoring is where someone encourages and supports individuals to maximise their potential and be the person that they want to be. Mentors can offer ideas and inspire individuals to achieve more and reach for the stars!

Start off by thinking of three people who could help you.

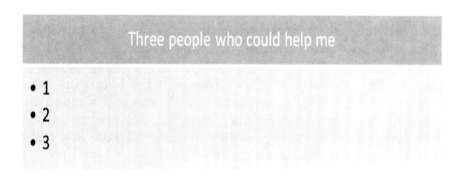

Three people who could help me

- 1
- 2
- 3

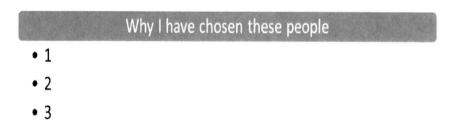

Why I have chosen these people

- 1
- 2
- 3

Great! You've already identified three people who could help you. Could any one of these people act as a mentor or coach? Your choice will depend on a number of factors: What do you want from them? What should they be like? Although most people will be flattered to act as a mentor, not everyone will feel that they have what it takes to be effective. Time commitment might be difficult and you will need someone who can at least agree to have contact with you on a fairly regular basis (although this is an area that you can agree on). Not everyone will feel that they have the right skills to do it.

But the key to success with targets is to have someone to motivate, encourage and give support and practical help.

In some reality TV programmes, boot camp refers to that very specific time when the contestant is assigned a mentor and linked to that person. It usually requires being taken to a place away from the normal surroundings, where the focus is to get ready for the task in hand. It might be to perform live in front of an audience (or in the case of ITV's 'The Biggest Loser' to lose as much weight as possible). In BBC One's 'The Voice UK', the coaches' primary goal is to develop their artists and to help them improve on their current talent. If they really wanted an artist on their team, the coaches would emphasize what they could offer the artist - whether it is Sir Tom Jones' extensive experience or will.i.am's great network and repertoire of artists. The coaches' pitch is the promise of sharing the secret of their success and how they can bring out the best in their team.

The goal is established and a series of activities are identified to help the individual achieve their goal. There is no secret about why that person is there. It is all about making the most effective action points to ensure success. New skills might be learnt or existing ones perfected. But remember - the target is **yours**. If someone else decides it for you, without consultation, you are less likely to achieve it. After all, it's you that has got to achieve it. So, go for something that YOU want to aim for and let the mentor be there to help you.

The choice of mentor has to be right, too. They have to understand the strengths and weaknesses of the person that they are working with. Going back to the talent-reality show format, a mentor has a very specific role. They are clear about the road ahead and what the goal is. Targets need to be fully understood. They also need to understand the needs of the contestant and establish the ways that they can effectively support them. It should focus on the individual.

Not all mentors will be the same. It will depend really on what you want and what they can offer. It can also depend on an activity. Training for a big race or weight loss, may require some tough love. Pushing people to achieve their goals can work well. At other times, a more gentle encouraging approach may be needed, especially if there has been a knock back. Whether it is helping you to write a CV or explore the many options available, a mentor can make a big difference.

Be clear on what might be helpful and also what they can offer. Many schools and colleges will know of people in business and across the community that are interested in mentoring young people. There might be local Education Business Partnerships where people volunteer to help young people. If you are thinking about higher education, some Universities may provide mentoring for students at school and college. Details can be found on University websites.

The key thing is that both parties are clear on what is expected. Be prepared to make a commitment and value the role mentoring can bring.

Target: I need help and support

Action: I need to identify a mentor/support network

Make it SMART

Ground rules

Your safety is crucial. Never ever agree to meet someone in your home, or their own home or car. It has to be in a public place and the usual safety rules apply. Be sensible and go through established mentoring routes. This could be through a programme at school with other students or from the business community. There is likely to be a teacher in school/college who will be involved in a mentoring programme. Email and online mentoring is also gaining in popularity, including forums on certain discussion areas. Again, the same safety rules should apply. When in doubt, check with a parent or teacher.

Establish what you want and ask someone to help you

In summary, the first thing is to get commitment to attend, participate and work with the coach.

At all times, remember that you are not auditioning for a new parent or someone to take over your life! Mentors should be constructive friends but it is **you** who makes the ultimate decisions about your life. The relationship needs to be a partnership with the focus on you. If you feel intimidated or overwhelmed, this is unlikely to be productive.

If having just one mentor sounds too scary at this moment, then think about getting a group of supporters together. Maybe a few of your friends could get together, especially if you have a common goal. If, for example, you wanted to look at applying to University, you might want to share your thoughts about different courses or Universities via a blog. There are plenty of forums out there where students talk about their experiences. Not all will be helpful though, but they are likely to mention things that don't always appear in prospectuses. Other websites such as wikijobs have comments and feedback for people going for interviews with different companies. Again, this can be helpful feedback and will be personal. Another idea is to set up a Facebook group or forum where people share ideas and tips to encourage. Think about any sports team. There is usually a main coach or trainer, but the team members support and encourage each other to achieve their common goal.

You might find it more helpful at this point to go to the part that reflects where you are at right now and read on from that point. But do carry on going through each of the following parts if you prefer to.

Action: Explore what I enjoy, what I am good at, what rocks my world.

Make it SMART.

Part 3

The weigh-in: where you are now, where you want to be and how are you going to get there

Start here if you are in year 9 or skip to Part 4 if you are in years 10 or 11. In years 12 and 13 you might want to go to Part 5.

Key Stage 3

Let's look at your current situation. If you are at Key Stage 3, then it is likely that your education has been decided for you. You will have a set number of lessons in Maths, English, Science, Geography, History and so on. However, half way though year 9, you are asked to make a decision about the range of subjects that you would like to take. Before you get too excited at the thought of never having to learn equations again, there are some rules put in place with subjects. In fact, there are some compulsory subjects. These are often Maths, English and Science, IT, PE and RE. These core subjects are often requirements for further courses, jobs or training.

So, let's work through your next steps.

Where I am now		
My current situation is	The decision I have to make is	My deadline is

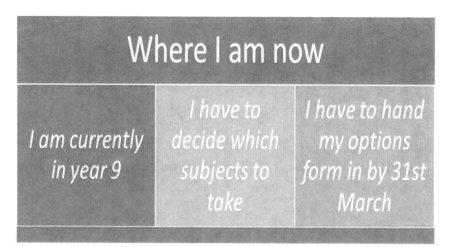

Making it easier

Rather than having a huge decision to make about choosing subjects, let's break it down even further into smaller bite size targets.

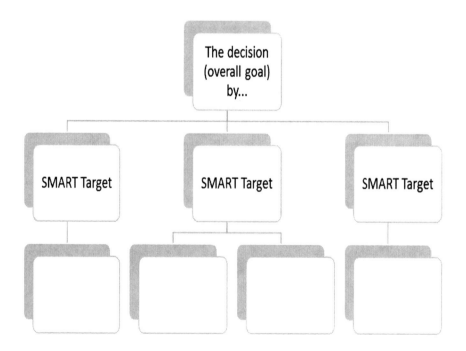

Start with what you would like to achieve and identify a goal. Break it down further still into smaller targets.

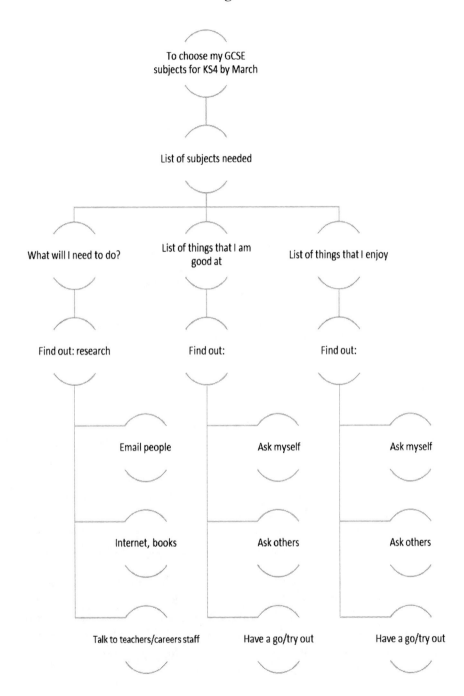

It might look daunting, but by breaking it into smaller chunks it means that things can be ticked off when they are done. Think how good you will feel then!

Finding out more:

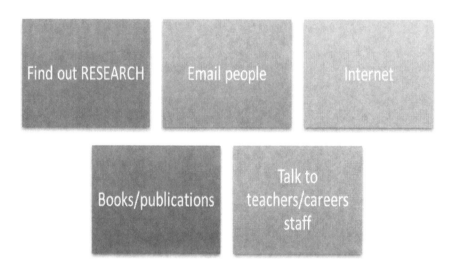

We can look at websites and find out information and in this book I have listed some great websites to get you started. You may have books in the school library or resources centre; ask the library staff to recommend some good ones to start with. Your school may also hold an options evening or careers event to talk you through how it works at your school. The subjects are usually arranged in groups that fit in around the timetable but also allow choice. Do talk to teachers and any careers staff if you would like more help with this.

You can also talk to people and find out what advice they have as well as what might be required. Does it look a bit scary? Think back to the **Just Me** and **Audition Stage**. There's a good chance that you have already found the answers that you need. Break it down into smaller chunks and ask your mentor or team of supporters to help you. You are not on your own.

Target: I need to get some voluntary/work experience or part time work

Action: *I need a CV for voluntary/work experience or applying for part time work*

Make it SMART.

Part 4

Years 10 and 11

Taster time

So, you've made those GCSE choices. Happy with them? Wished you'd thought about it a little more? Maybe you've really got into some of the subjects and starting to explore some job/course ideas linked to the subject you are already taking. School, colleges and local training organisations will start to take a real interest in you, because at the end of year 11, you can decide to change your course of study. Perhaps your school doesn't offer a particular subject or course of study. Maybe it doesn't even have a sixth form. At this point, please remember that there are lots of options for you to pick from.

Think of it like the various price comparison websites that are promoted on TV (usually with cute animals and catchy jingles). They present all of the different options for you, based on the information that you put in. Some will be better suited to your needs than others.

But when it comes to your future, it's you who will identify what suits your needs and is the best product for you. This can be done by applying the same examples in year 9 from the previous part.

Rather than having a huge decision to make about choosing subjects, let's break it down even further into smaller bite size targets.

What you might want to focus on is finding about courses.

Part 5

Finding out about courses

If you are looking at a subject linked in with a certain career choice, you will need to make sure that you have the correct information. In the first instance, I suggest that you talk to somebody who is trained in careers advice and can direct you to the best resources to talk through your ideas. If this isn't available start off by looking at some good websites I've recommended in this book. If you are looking at certain job areas, then you will probably find that there is a professional body or organisation that is linked to it. For example, if you are interested in jobs in health, you could check out the NHS website www.nhscareers.nhs.uk, before looking at more specific careers such as the Chartered Society of Physiotherapists www.csp.org.uk. You may even find out about the latest news and events which will help you to decide. They will usually have very good careers information and mention good subjects to take and work experience that you will need.

Part 6

Making the most of work experience

But what is it really like to be…a physiotherapist, for example? Again, a great way forward is to talk to one and if possible, gain some great experience in that area. It can be difficult to get work experience in hospitals or the care sector, but you may be able to work shadow someone for a day (which means watching what they do, without undertaking any of the activities). Your school may organise work experience placements and have a list of placements or ask you to choose or find out your own. In this case, look at areas which are closely related to the job you are interested in, but be prepared to be flexible. You can learn a lot about caring skills from work experience in a care home. The purpose is to find out if you enjoy it and whether your interests and skills are being used.

Have you ever watched *'The Apprentice'* or *'Young Apprentice'* on BBC One? The contestants are brought together to share the same house and are competing for the ultimate prize. It is financial investment in a contestant's business idea which Lord Sugar believes will make him money. As a successful businessman and entrepreneur, he is keen to spot talent as well as see an opportunity to make money. Check out previous episodes on YouTube.

Each week the candidates are put into teams and are set a challenge to complete within a deadline. One person volunteers or is nominated to be a project manager and as a team they work together to win the task and beat the other team.

That's the idea anyway. What it often shows is that strong personalities, poor communication and lack of planning sometimes get in the way and that teams can break down.

It can be highly entertaining watching the candidates desperately trying to sell a product or impress a retailer but the really interesting part for me is the situation at the end when the teams end up in the boardroom. Lord Sugar and his two aides comment on what they have observed and evaluate the situation. The candidates are encouraged to draw their own conclusions about their performances as well as their team. When the spotlight is turned on them, it requires quick thinking to identify their strengths, skills and contributions. Their immediate goal is survival to the next stage so they can draw closer to the eventual prize. The activity might have been to produce a new food product, but it's the learning that's important.

With work experience you may not get the dream opportunity or placement, but I want to encourage you to see it as part of a much bigger process, like in 'The Apprentice'. You can learn an enormous amount about yourself as well as the area of work. It also demonstrates commitment and your willingness to train for a future goal. And that is all part of the boot camp experience.

Before you go on work experience:

What do you hope to get from this experience?

Knowledge about the placement...

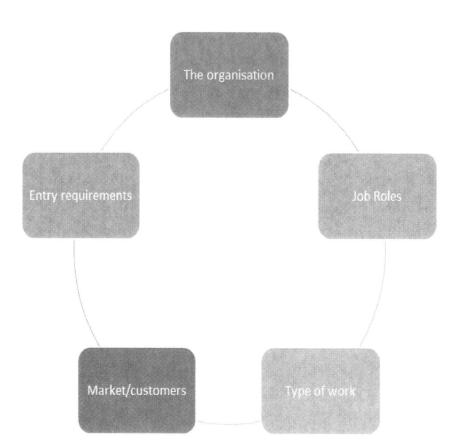

Knowledge about myself...

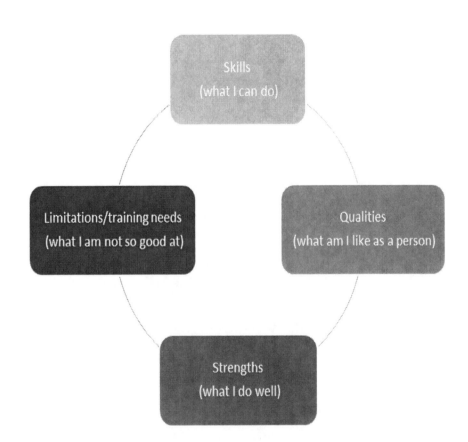

My action plan for the work experience placement is:

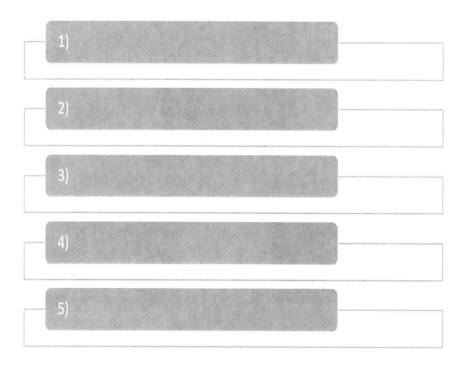

1)

2)

3)

4)

5)

Part 7

Getting experience

Creating a CV for voluntary/work experience or part time work when you are in years 10-12

A CV for part time jobs or work experience

CV, 'curriculum vitae' or 'the story of my life' is your opportunity to sell yourself in no more than two pages of A4. There are literally hundreds of books in the UK focusing on CVs which give templates and examples of the perfect CV. But what works for you, may not necessarily work for the person sat next to you.

Think of your CV as an advert – if the average amount of time an employer spends reading a CV is around twenty seconds then you need to get it right. A CV is an edited and relevant version of your life, not your whole life story!

A good advert, whether it is on TV, radio or in a magazine, grabs the attention of the passer-by. Catchy jingles and distinctive images work – how many of us could name McDonald's slogan and hum the tune, even if we don't like them?

Your CV is therefore your advert and there are two very important elements to understand.

Firstly, you need to know who your market is. In other words, who will be reading your CV?

Have a go... jot down where you might want to work for a part time job. Say, for example, you would like to work in a newsagents...

Start off with what you think happens at a newsagents.

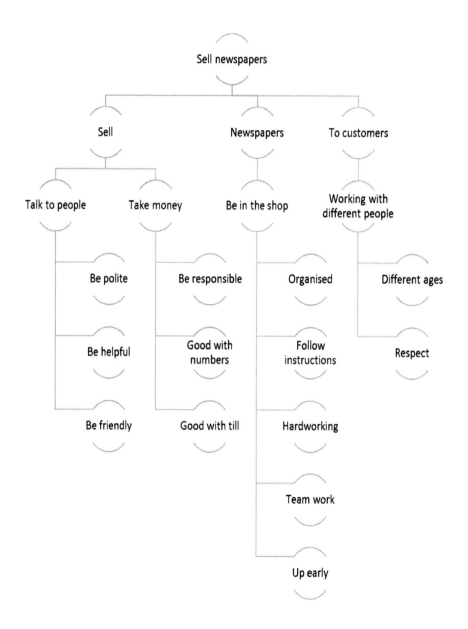

Just from this example you can see that the newsagent's manager will be looking for someone who:

Can talk to people

Be polite

Be friendly

Take money

Show responsibility

Be organised

Follow instructions

Up early

Hardworking

Be a team worker

Shows respect

Can work with different people and different age

The second part of the advert is to write a list of *how* you match up to this list:

What I do in school

- helping teachers, work experience, helping out in sports days, clubs and activities
- subjects taken

What I do outside school

- sports activities, hobbies, interests, scouts, guides, and youth clubs

Have you ever done any fundraising, such as *Sport Relief* or *Children in Need?* Helping out at a charity event can show that you are helpful, friendly, a good team player and trustworthy.

Ask your friends and family too. How would they describe you? Think back to the **Audition Stage**. Remember, it is down to you to let the employer know all of the things that you can do well (skills) as well as what you are like as a person (qualities and soft skills). You need to tempt them, in their very busy lives, to want to find out more about you. You need to speak their language, work out what they want and show them that you have it.

Now that you've got a list of key selling points, you are ready to start your CV

Throughout my work life, I have seen literally thousands of CVs – some good, but generally most are not good because they miss the point. They don't see the CV as a potential advert or a way to 'showcase' the best skills and experiences. Rather, they tend to bore the reader, chop and change style, follow random patterns or contain many distractions. They believe that because a CV literally means 'life story' they must include everything about their life, from the names of their pets through to every holiday they have ever been on!

Ready to write a great CV for work experience or part time work?

Grab your list of positive achievements and skills that we talked about earlier.

Get two pieces of paper.

Start off with your contact details. You don't have to include your middle name unless you really want to. If you include your email address make sure it isn't cheeky or likely to offend the employer! If you give your home phone number, let everyone you live with know that you have given it out. But if you give out your mobile number, remember that you are giving them permission to call you at anytime and anywhere. Always answer politely. You don't want to ruin your chances with a rude *"What?!"* Also, don't forget to have a clean answer phone message.

Having covered your basic contact details we can now look at your advert. Don't worry about putting your date of birth or nationality. You don't have to make a big deal about your age - it's your skills and experiences that are important. BUT there are laws and regulations that exist to protect you. There will be some jobs that you can't do until you reach a certain age. Your school will know this information - it will usually be provided by an Education Welfare Officer or the teacher responsible for work experience. An employer will usually be able to work out your age by when you take/took your GCSEs at school but when asked by an employer, never lie about your age.

The advert

A personal profile can help showcase your best bits. You don't want to write too much but three sentences work best. These are the 3 S's:

Situation

Selling

Seeking

Your first sentence should explain your current **situation**.

"GCSE student with experience of working with people and fundraising."

Your second sentence should identify key words to 'sell' your best attributes.

"Hardworking, community minded, friendly and willing team member."

Finally, let the reader know what you want.

"Seeking opportunities to work with the public in a sales environment."

If you were using this to apply for work experience or you are interested in this career area in the future, then you could write:

"Long term career goal is to work in the retail sector and keen to gain experience and work as part of a team as soon as possible."

Qualifications

If you have taken these exams and have qualifications then you could start your CV with these.

Start with the most recent first and put the dates on the right hand side. It's a clever little trick to keep the dates here – it means that the reader focuses on **what** you have done rather than getting distracted by **when** you did it.

When it comes to GCSEs, you don't have to list every single subject and its grade. To save space you could put instead:

"9 GCSEs all at grades A-C, including English (B), Maths (C) and Science (B,B)"

But, if you want to draw attention to certain GCSEs or you are worried that you will have very little on your CV, then go for it and list them.

If you have taken an alternative qualification, such as a diploma or short course, do put it down, but be ready to explain what it means.

If you haven't taken your GCSEs yet, then you can list all of the subjects that you are currently studying and when you will be taking exams in them. There should be start and finish dates so readers of your CV know that you haven't got them yet.

If you have had some work experience, now is your time to shine

Work experience isn't just the week or two weeks that school organises. It could also be part time jobs from babysitting and newspaper delivery through to stable hand and shop assistant.

It might be helpful to think of this section as Work Related Experience. Write down any opportunity where you have had the chance to learn about the world of work and what you got out of it.

Schools are required to provide opportunities in the curriculum for all students to learn about work and what it means to develop skills. Industry days, visit to employers, activities with a wide variety of organisations can all be included.

Under this heading: **Work Related Experience** you could have further headings such as:

Employment

Voluntary work

Business Related Activities

This works well if you have **lots of different** types of experience. But if you want to, you can keep it all under the one heading. Remember this is your CV and so you can decide what suits you best.

Under the section **Work Related Experience** you should keep things snappy and skills focused. Let's look at this example below:

Example: helping out with the school's *'Children in Need'* event.

The best way to approach this is to identify the **key skills** developed.

First of all, jot down what you did.

"I helped go around to each class with a friend to collect money from everybody who had turned up to school in fancy dress. I then helped my friends to bake cakes and sell them to students at break time. The money was counted up with a teacher present to check the money. I had to make sure that we reimbursed the cake bakers for their ingredients, with the rest of the money going to Children in Need."

Grab a highlighter or underline the key skills. They are all verbs.

"I **helped** go around to each class with a friend to **collect** money from everybody who had tuned up to school in fancy dress. I then **helped** my friends to **bake** cakes and **sell** them to students at break time. The money was **counted** up with a teacher present to check the money. I had to make sure that we **reimbursed** the cake bakers for their ingredients, with the rest of the money going to Children in Need."

What did you do?

Try and identify three key skills.

Financial responsibility from collecting donations, checking money raised and ensuring payment is made.

Encouraging participation in fund raising activities from cake baking through to fancy dress.

Effective teamwork with both students and teachers.

Start to piece it all together.

What I did? Fundraiser for Children in Need

When? November 2012

Where? Bramshall High School

Add these three points:

1. Financial responsibility from collecting donations, checking money raised and ensuring payment is made.

2. Encouraging participation in fund raising activities from cake baking through to fancy dress.

3. Effective teamwork with both students and teachers.

Repeat this activity with every example in this section.

The next section of the CV allows you to *showcase* your best achievement or proudest moments.

This heading will be **'Additional skills and Achievements'**. It could be class rep, treasurer of the film club, and award for the best design at the year 10 industry day. Don't forget activities outside school, such as sport, leisure or community activities. Do you have any unique talents? Black belt in judo? Speak another language? Basic sign language? First Aid?

You probably know more about IT than most employers, so don't forget to include IT skills, such as awareness of software. If you have a driving licence don't forget to include this too.

How interesting are you?

In the **interests** section of the CV have a brief list – not too many details, but enough to give a flavour of what you do in your spare time. Remember who is going to read this CV and that you are looking to impress them. So perhaps putting 'playing computer games all day' might not be the best thing. Saying you are 'competent in multimedia, computer literate and keep a blog', shows some benefit to the employer.

Finally, you have the opportunity to add the name and **contact details** of two people who are not your family or friends, but who can provide a reference or answer questions about you. You must get their permission first and ask them for their contact details. Most people choose a teacher or someone who knows them for work experience or a part time job. It could even be a sports coach or youth leader.

But if you are running out of space or would rather not include the details of the two referees, then that's okay, just write *'References available on request'* and get ready to provide those details when asked.

Part 8

CV format for work experience or part time job

Name and Contact Details

Personal Profile

1. Explain your current situation

2. Key words to 'sell'

3. Seeking opportunity

Education and Qualifications

(Starting with the most recent first)

Where you studied (dates)

What you studied

Work Related Experience

Employment

Voluntary work

Business Related Activities

Additional skills and achievements

Interests

References

It's usual to include two, one from education (school/college) and another from either work experience, employment, a part time job, voluntary work or a group.

If you are in year 10, it might look something like this. If you want to see another CV then take a look at the CV Examples page under VIP Access at www.whatrocksyourworld.com.

Alex Edge

42 White Cliff Way

Bramshall, Staffordshire

ST44 8OO

Alexedge800@hotmail.co.uk

0144 800 800

Personal Profile

GCSE student with experience of working with people and fundraising. Hardworking, community minded, friendly and willing team member. Seeking opportunities to work with the public in a sales environment.

Education and Qualifications

Bramshall High School, Bramshall   2009-2014

GCSEs in English Language, English Literature, Mathematics

Chemistry, Biology, Physics (Double award Science)

Business Studies, IT Certificate of competency

History, Religious Studies, French

Work Related Experience

Employment

Babysitting for primary school aged child   **2013 - present**

- Responsible for ensuring safety and well-being of the child

Voluntary work

Fundraiser for Children in Need - Bramshall High School   **Nov 2012**

- Financial responsibility, collecting donations, checking money raised and ensuring payment is made

- Encouraging participation in fund raising activities from cake baking though to fancy dress

- Effective teamwork with both students and teachers

Business Related Activities

Marketing Assistant Young Enterprise - Bramshall High School   **2013 - present**

- Assisted market research of new product across school

- Supported social media marketing via Facebook and Twitter

Additional skills and achievements

Year 10 class rep and awarded merit for school community award

Nominated to represent school at Regional Young Enterprise competition

Conversational French

British Sign Language

Fully competent in practical application of range of IT packages, including Microsoft Word, Excel, PowerPoint

Interests

Social media, design, cross country running and charity fundraising

References

Mr Kenneth	Mrs Dillon
Bramshall High School	Dillons News Agent
Windy End	1, The Square
Bramshall	Bramshall
ST44 1AA	ST44 1BB

If you are in **year 11**, you should draw attention to any GCSEs that you have taken early, such as in year 10. Also include the subjects that you are studying now and will be taking exams in. You will also have had more opportunities for work experience which should be emphasised.

If you are in **year 12**, you will have your GCSEs already and be taking new qualifications. You may find it more helpful to look at the CVs in Part 26.

Part 9

Finding part time work

So, what's the best way to approach employers for part time work? Did you know that many vacancies are never advertised? They are often filled before you even knew that they were looking for staff. Here are some good ways to approach them.

Ask around. Let people know that you are looking for a part time job. Got friends who have jobs? Let them know that you are looking for one. Family are also a useful place to network. Get those that know you asking around and listen to their suggestions. Facebook, Twitter and other social networking sites are also great ways to get your message out.

Getting others to do all the hard work for you is not the answer! Take control for yourself and let employers know what you are looking for. You can do this in a number of ways. What you need to remember though is that busy employers will notice you very quickly for either the right or wrong reasons.

Some jobs will be advertised in shop windows or in the local press. There are vacancy sections in newspapers as well as the many job websites. But remember that many will be for over 16s, so check that you are eligible to apply.

Getting first impressions right

Here are a few things to get right beforehand to show you in the best light. Firstly, check that your letter and CV have the correct spelling and grammar.

Make sure you get the right name and address and spell it correctly. Irritate an employer in seconds and your hard work is likely to end up in the bin.

Get someone else to check the spelling and grammar for you and remove any slang or text speak. You would be amazed at how many letters I have seen that include 'gr8t', 'I' and 'wd'!

In one side of A4, you can show that you are keen, good at communicating, honest and ready for hard work.

"Give me a job!" is unlikely to get you that crucial interview, but being clear and polite is. Remember that in approximately 20 seconds an employer is going to form an opinion of you and decide whether you are going to be short listed and make it down to the final round. These judges can be harsh!

Generally speaking it is best to type, particularly if you have atrocious handwriting, but for some jobs they may want to see evidence of your writing. You don't need to buy fancy paper, but make sure that it is white/ivory and clean.

Part 10

Covering letters

Dear ???

If possible, find out who the manager is. Some organisations such as shops may have a department that deals with enquiries, often called 'Human Resources' or 'Personnel'. If you are unsure of their name, it is okay to begin it as *"Dear Sir or Madam"*, but make sure that you follow the standard conventions of letter writing.

Ideally your letter should have no more than four paragraphs.

State clearly **why you are writing to them**. Is it in response to a vacancy? If so, say when and where you saw it. For example, *"in response to your advert for sales assistant at White's bakery, as advertised in Bramshall Post Office on 21st August 2013."*

Or are you checking to see if there are any vacancies? For example, *"I am writing to enquire as to the possibility of any vacancies for Saturday work at your shop."*

In your next paragraph explain **WHY** you are writing to them. Show you have done a bit of research, not too much, but enough to let the employer know that you are interested in **them**. If you saw the TV programme *'The Apprentice'* you will have seen that some candidates failed to impress the interview panel by not knowing anything about their potential employer, Lord Sugar.

So, what have you got to offer, in other words, **WHY YOU**? Give a brief overview of what you have done before or why you think you would be good at this work. For example: *"From my work experience at WHSmith, I showed that I could talk comfortably to customers and help them purchase goods, being polite and courteous. Helping out with the very popular school tuck shop has meant that I can work as part of a team under pressure. At school I have been described by my teachers as being helpful and a mature member of my class."*

63

Finally, **thank them** for taking the time to read your letter and remind them of your availability for an interview, or even the dates you are looking at. If you promise to contact them at a later date then make sure that you follow it up. If you can afford to and you are using snail mail, you may wish to include a stamped addressed envelope.

It should therefore look something like this...

Dear......... (Better to include their name. If not, use 'Sir or Madam')

First paragraph

In response to your job advert for shop assistant at your newsagents, as advertised in Bramshall Post Office, please find enclosed a copy of my CV, detailing my skills and experiences.

OR

I am writing to enquire as to whether you have any opportunities for part time work at your company.

Second paragraph

I am keen to work for your shop as you are at the heart of the community and well known for your excellent customer service.

Third paragraph

From my voluntary work/work experience/previous part time jobs I have gained experience in... had the opportunity to... I enjoy... excel at... keen to... (use key words to identify your successes and strengths).

Final paragraph

Thank you for taking the time to read my letter and CV and I look forward to hearing from you soon.

Yours sincerely (if you know their name), yours faithfully (if you don't).

Sending an email

If you have an email address, you should still follow the same format as the above covering letter, but you don't need to include their address. It is much better to have four paragraphs in your email as above, rather than a sentence saying *"Please see attached CV"*. If you prefer you can also add the covering letter and CV as attachments. First impressions really do count, so a politely worded email, stating why you are writing to them will go a long way. Make sure that your email address is appropriate, as I've mentioned before, avoid humorous/rude names!

Remember that this really is your opportunity to shine and let someone know what you have to offer.

Part 11

Talking to employers directly

If you have the time and you feel confident enough to do it, meeting someone face to face can really create a positive impression. It shows that you have initiative and are keen to introduce yourself. Don't forget to give them your CV and include a covering letter as well so they will know at a later date why you left your CV with them. It can be nerve-wracking talking to people we don't know, so preparing what to say beforehand can help. Remember you can make a positive impression, even before you have said anything! It is said that much of communication is silent. In other words it is our body language that conveys so much! A positive impression can be created by:

Making eye contact: look at the other person's eyes without staring. This shows that you are interested and engaging in a conversation. Look at it the other way - if someone approaches you but stares at the floor, you will feel that they really don't want to talk to you.

Shake hands: a firm but not too hard shake - we don't want broken fingers!

You can also appear more confident by how you stand. Standing tall and putting your shoulders back instantly adds height and can help you breathe better. You are less likely to feel nervous as your lungs can fill with more breath.

Be a people watcher and look at how people's body language can influence your impression of them. Just looking around a shopping centre and watching people about their daily business is a great way to watch body language and see how they appear.

Smiling can make such a difference. Look at yourself in a mirror to see what a difference body language can make. If you want to look into this in more detail then go to the **Showcase Final** section where body language is covered at greater depth.

Part 12

Learning from work experience

What I have learnt from my work experience:

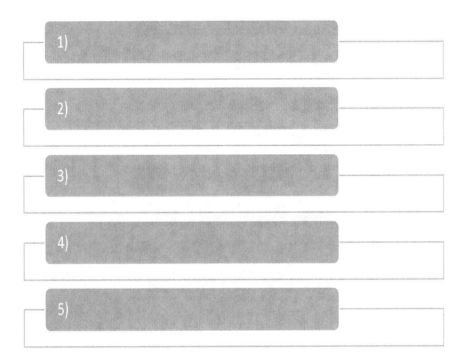

My greatest achievement was:

The thing that "rocked my world" during the placement was:

The thing that I didn't enjoy was:

The list of skills, achievements and experiences I can include in future CVs and applications:

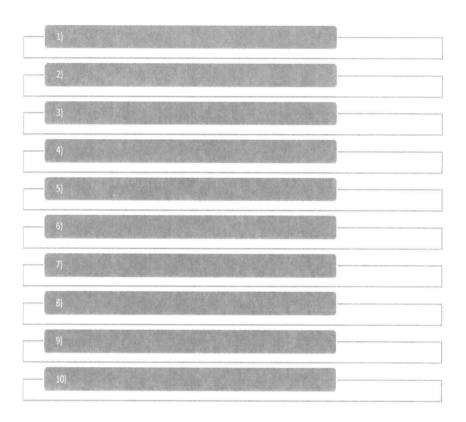

You can think about what you have learnt from your work experience, what you enjoyed and what you didn't enjoy. Reflecting on this will give you insight into your skills and achievements (and also help you to write your CV). If you have done work experience was there anything you did which really rocked your world?

Try to get feedback from the placement's supervisor. Don't forget to ask them if they would be happy to include a testimonial about you. They might even provide a reference for you in the future. How about adding some of this to your personal blog? Keep all of this as evidence of your great commitment to training in **Boot Camp**.

Part 13

After GCSEs. Decision time - study or training

Whether you like it or not, you will have to make a decision about your next step beyond GCSEs. If your school has a Sixth Form, they will set entry requirements, probably with specific grades for you to continue your studies. Local colleges may also run similar courses, as well as new ones. Work experience may be offered as part of the courses. Some will be very practical, with very little classroom teaching and essay writing. Others will be taught by teachers or lecturers, who set frequent essays or assignments with regular coursework deadlines. When looking at the huge selection on offer, you will need to think about the following:

Your career goal – do you need specific subjects or can you keep your options open? As before, do your research and find out the facts. Ask the subject/course teachers, but always check it with other sources, such as professional bodies or up to date careers websites. If you are looking at University, they may specify a certain course or subjects. Be savvy. When in doubt, go back to your mentors/support group.

What brings out the best in you? If you hate writing essays, presenting ideas and research, then A‘ levels in History, English and Law are probably not for you. But if your passion is design, being practical and trying things out, then Graphic Design or Design and Technology may be for you. Ask your teachers where your strengths lie. Use the ideas in this book.

What do people who do my course go on to do? Establishing the success rate and what people do next is vital. Ask the teachers what courses or jobs people move on to. Does it open many doors? By law, they will have to collect data on what students do after their studies, so ask the questions. It's your future, so do the research now. **Boot Camp** is about putting the energy in now, to reap the rewards later.

Got the picture? Know what you need to do? Write your training plan now and don't forget to identify who can help you. Start off with your overall target and break it down into smaller targets. Ask your mentor for specific targets that you might need more help with.

Part 14

Have a go/try it out: creating a training plan

Your training plan could therefore be a number of activities to get into shape and ready for the **Showcase Final**. With a plan and some targets you will be able to impress the judges.

Get SMART with your targets:

Target: I need to know what I want to do

'I will have at least two career ideas written down before I go to the Sixth Form College open evening in January.

Each career idea will have the entry requirements written next to it and identify subjects taken at College.

Before the open evening I will have written down three questions to ask the subject teachers and the Careers Adviser. I will ask my mentor to suggest a good question to ask and to check my questions.

At the open evening I will talk to subject teachers and write down their answers.

After the open evening, in the following week, I will talk about any action points I have with my mentor.'

Top Tip: To make the most of your time at an open evening, plan who you want to talk to beforehand. You'll create a great impression if you are prepared, you'll make the most of your time. You will feel great being in control and getting answers to your questions.

Add here:

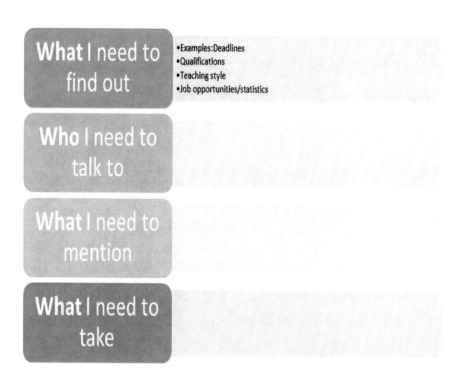

Part 15

Year 12: University/training/work: what next?

You thought that it was hard to narrow down subjects for GCSE and A' level? The next step will require you to thoroughly assess where you are at now and what you've learnt about yourself. It also means identifying any gaps.

Boot Camp is ensuring that you are ready for the **Showcase Final**, whether it's applying for a job or a place at University.

Start off by reviewing any original training plans and the milestones achieved along the way.

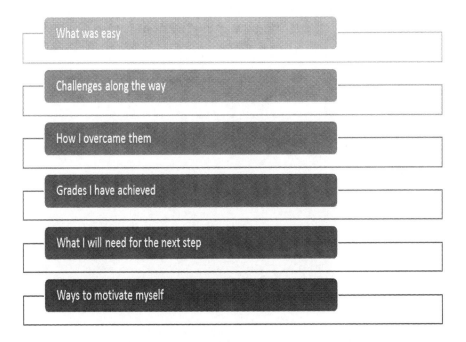

What was easy

Challenges along the way

How I overcame them

Grades I have achieved

What I will need for the next step

Ways to motivate myself

If you have hit problems with previous training plans, talk to your mentor/support groups. How might you improve?

Boot Camp is the **preparation stage**. It's about trying things out. It's about asking lots of questions.

By years 12 and 13, you should have some work experience/shadowing under your belt. Whether it's organised by your school or college, or you've organised it yourself you will have developed some new understanding of that career area, as well as new skills and knowledge. If you are arranging your own work experience, please seek guidelines from a Careers Adviser/teacher, or someone who has responsibility for work experience. The priority is to be safe, so some placements may be excluded and there will certainly be implications for insurance, so both you, and the people you are working with, are safe and protected.

If you haven't any experience, what's stopping you? Part time jobs are not just an excellent way of getting cash, but also great evidence to prove you are developing certain key skills and qualities. **Showcase Final** is serious. When the spotlight is on you, you will be relying on all the training you have gained in **Boot Camp**.

Part 16

How committed are you? Have you got what it takes?

In the boot camp phase of reality shows, such as *X Factor* the contestants are usually taken away from their home environment. Contact with friends and family is reduced to occasional phone calls. The training plan is agreed and 100% commitment is required. If that commitment isn't given, then contestants often doubt why they are there, struggle with the activities and want to go home.

Now, I am not suggesting anything so drastic! In fact, I want your friends and family to be there for you. But, I do want you to be focused. I am not suggesting you lock yourself away and only emerge for your exams. What I want you to focus on is:

1. Being committed to getting the best experience for you.

2. Making the most of opportunities that come your way.

Earlier on I talked about how some people 'found' their careers. You will have probably discovered that many people have planned what they wanted to do in the future. They had a plan and stuck to it. But as I mentioned about my sister, sometimes the plan doesn't work out as originally planned, **but it still works out**. The point is that life can present many exciting opportunities along the way and the key to success is recognising when it's a good opportunity. So, in the *X Factor*, one of the mentors may suggest a contestant tries a new song or style. It may work or it may not. **But it does mean that the contestant has been exposed to a new thing and learnt something about themselves.** Between ages 16-18, in particular, there will be plenty of opportunities to get involved. Your school and college may be looking for volunteers to help with younger students, in learning or sport. There'll be parties or fundraising events to organise. Or there'll be committees or opportunities to be a student representative. See these opportunities as adding value to your experience. You'll meet new people and learn new things. And it might just light a spark or give you an idea.

Part 17

University: what is on offer and getting informed

When you start to explore University courses, you will see that there is no such thing as the typical degree. Undergraduate courses refer to those where you will be awarded a degree on successful completion of that course. Do check the length of the course. While the majority of courses are for three years, some will be for four. Some courses such as medicine or veterinary science, will be at least five years long.

At the **research stage**, the following checklist should provide some good starting points.

Length of course.

How it is taught (lectures, seminars, tutorials, workshops, on line programmes).

Who will teach it? Are they from industry? What is their area of expertise? What areas have they research in?

What support is available to me? (E.g. learning support, finance, careers advice, counselling and placements).

Where will I be based?

What do people go on to do after taking their course? What are the statistics?

What are the main careers areas? What further courses do people go on to study?

Is this course accredited or approved by a professional organisation or career?

Match up the answers to what you already know about your learning style, in other words, how and where you learn best. What have you learnt about yourself so far?

It might mean a bit of digging around. By going to www.ucas.com you can search for courses by broad subject areas, specific course titles or codes. You can also search focussing on certain areas of the country and length of course.

To start with, keep your search broad, and then reduce the list down as you do your research. **Always** check behind the title. 'Film Studies' could be a theoretical course looking at the sociological impact of films and the impact of political beliefs in post war America. Not much use if you were hoping for a practical hands on course that will show you how to be an effective producer, director or trained in camera use.

Take a closer look

If you are in doubt about any course, go to the website of that particular institution and find your course. Study the details of the course and follow any links that they suggest. Attend an open day at the University, which are usually organised on a regular basis. **Please, please, please check out the University!**

Having worked in Universities for over eight years, I am constantly amazed when students confess they had never checked out the University campus, where the lectures were held or even the accommodation. If you are just looking at websites and prospectuses, it is not enough. They are designed to look good and tempt you. They are always made to look as though the sun always shines. They are unlikely to show you the less glamorous parts! Also check the location of your course. It might not even be on the main campus, but over a bus ride away and this might mean early morning or late night travel. If that's important to you, then find it out now, and not when you arrive on your first day at University.

Having worked at two Universities in the same city, I've seen parents and students confused as to which University they are really at!

You can also email admission tutors. Their job is to make sure that prospective students are fully informed about the course, so they can make a well informed decision. If you can't find the answer to your question from the website or prospectus then do drop them a line. Because they are very busy, they'll do their best to reply as soon as they can, but they won't be impressed if your answers could be clearly found on the website. If they can help, then they will, as it is in their best interest. But you can't try to sway them as to why they should pick you. That will be done through your personal statement, your predicted (or actual grades) as well as at interview (if this is part of their process).

Target: I want to go University but I don't know what I want to do.

Action: *I need a list of University courses that are right for me.*

Training plans written? Ticked off your checklist? You've done the research...

Take your pulse... how are you doing in **Boot Camp?**

Part 18

Insider information: checking the small print. Do the numbers add up?

Statistics on every course are collected to look at what people go on to do having completed a course. Maybe you've had a phone call or questionnaire in the post and wondered why they need to know. Basically it is a legal requirement of course providers to ensure there is a collection of destinations data and to allow it to be available. It can help to show trends such as unemployment rate and the areas that people go into. It can also reveal average starting salaries and the range of salaries earned. When it comes to applying for courses in school sixth forms or colleges, the institution itself will have the facts and figures. When you ask questions about programmes of study, do ask about job types, salaries and unemployment rate. You need to know what the situation was like over the last few years.

It can be a bit like when you read a review of the latest album by an artist or band. It is important to look behind the story and see the big picture. For example, with music reviews, if the reviewer loves or hates the person or genre, it's likely to reflect in the review. If the reviewer is a huge fan of Lady Gaga, there's a good chance that they will review her latest album favourably.

When it comes to destinations data, it's important to put it into context and see the bigger picture. What was the job market like at the time? Have other courses been affected? When companies need to save money they usually stop recruiting until their financial position looks much stronger. When the financial markets crashed in 2007/8 many people were made redundant without notice and recruitment stopped for some time. Because recruiting wasn't a priority many talented and qualified people struggled to get work even though their qualifications had been excellent. This meant that the unemployment figures were much higher for students looking for their first job.

When it comes to looking at Universities you can compare different courses against each other. Again it's important to look at the bigger picture. There are a number of league tables produced each year by different organisations who look at the data and then assess it based on different criteria. Not surprisingly, the way that the data is looked at means that each version has a slightly different emphasis and different charts. It's a bit like comparing the download chart with the official top 40 or the chart show.

I've included a few websites for you to research on your **Boot Camp** training plan. You might want to start with universityleaguetables.co.uk. They provide comparisons of different Universities and different courses. And just as the music reviewers or the *Top Gear* presenters hold very different views, so will these league tables:

www.thecompleteuniversityguide.co.uk

www.topuniversityleaguetables.co.uk

www.guardian.co.uk/education/universityguide

Part 19

Stay SMART and working with your mentor

As in all boot camps, regular feedback from your supporters is vital. Plan to meet regularly with a mentor and be prepared to talk about some of the obstacles you may have faced as well as the progress made. If you can't meet in person, or have agreed to update via email or text, make sure that you identify the positives and every bit of success you have had. When things haven't gone according to plan explain ways in which you could overcome them next time. If it works for you, consider writing a blog. It could be for your eyes only, a select few or the whole world. Looking back you will be able to see how you've undertaken activities to get you ready for the big applications or interviews.

Try to stay on task. If you miss target dates agree new ones. Make them **achievable** and **realistic** as these are crucial parts of target setting. If you realise you are over-ambitious or even too cautious then adjust your targets. The emphasis has to be on training yourself to work towards something you want. However it is no good sprinting hard if you've set yourself a marathon of targets. Pace yourself and be realistic about what you can achieve in a certain time. Burnout isn't going to be helpful.

Keeping up with the competition

Although the focus of **Boot Camp** is about you and your personal goals, every person going through this process knows that there are others who are facing the same trials. They have similar dreams and goals and they also aim to be 100% prepared for the **Showcase Final**. *X Factor* mentors will often have a group of mentees. The competitors are all looking to achieve their goal and be winners, but they will certainly be watching each other and trying to work out secrets of success and get top tips. The problem with certain talent contests is that there is just one winner. But if we take your year group at school or college there is a good chance that you'll be looking at a wide variety of options. You might want to share your training plan ideas with others and find out how they got work experience, for example. Visits to colleges and universities could be shared giving you the chance to talk about your experiences together.

Be savvy. Find a way of being informed and fully updates about the **Showcase Final.**

Part 20

Who are the judges and what are they looking for?

If it's a particular course at university and it's linked to a job area make sure that you've done your research on that subject or profession. Say, for example, you are interested in finance. You might want to go into banking, accountancy, insurance or tax. How would you prove to the judges that you've trained hard in researching these areas and are aware of the latest news? Reading *The Financial Times* and finance pages of newspapers and watching the news will keep you updated. But how about going to the websites of certain companies or professional organisations linked to these areas? Most will have career sections that talk about career routes and how they recruit. More likely there will be news and events pages. This doesn't just apply to the world of finance - many organisations will use the internet to communicate with their customers as well as potential employees.

Want to be one of the first to get their news? Then follow them on Twitter. Many organisations are realising the powerful impact a tweet can have. Sign up for Twitter and who knows? They might start following you.

Part 21

What does the world know about you?

Public Relations (PR) and publicity are crucial parts of the big plan to prepare the final candidates for the big **Showcase Final**. Stories will get out in the press creating a stir with exclusives. It is usually part of a campaign to tempt people to start following certain individuals and to check them out.

So what does the world know about you? Would Google find you? Got a Facebook account? Bingo! If I wanted to find you, chances are I could also see those dodgy photos of you on holiday, as well as find out your musical tastes. Many recruiters will look at your digital footprint or digital dirt by Googling you, checking out Facebook or even looking at YouTube. Though it's great to keep in touch with your mates and show your allegiance to various Facebook groups, would you want your dream employer checking you out in this way? The easiest thing to do is to change your privacy settings. You might also want to remove some tags of you in photos. If you are looking to join career areas that require you to sign up to a professional code of conduct, such as the police, teaching or health careers, keeping a good profile will be important.

You can, however, use the internet and social media in a positive way. If people do want to search and find things out, make a positive impression and create a professional image of yourself. Be savvy and be creative.

One of the best things that you can do is create a website that does the PR for you. Put your IT and design skills to good use by creating a webpage that allows you to showcase your work experience, skills and experiences. It could contain a blog about your work experience (but always protect people's identity and confidentiality) or it could be pictures of charity and volunteering activities. It could contain a mini-resumé, clips of films you've made or pictures of your artwork. Keep your personal contact details, such as your address or phone number private, but do encourage people to contact you via an email address. Spend time on getting it right and you've promoted yourself to a worldwide audience.

Part 22

Updating your training plan

Have a go/try it out

Your training plan could therefore include a number of activities to get you into shape and ready for the **Showcase Final**.

Get SMART with your targets:

Specific   Measurable   Achievable   Realistic   Time

Targets can be written down, made public on a blog or a social networking site, or be known only to the person that wrote them. But when goals are set, they can be ticked off when they have been achieved. Decide **when** you will record progress and the **deadline** to achieve them. **Where** and **how** you record them is your choice, but make sure you talk to your mentor about this, as they will help you review them and offer support to their progress.

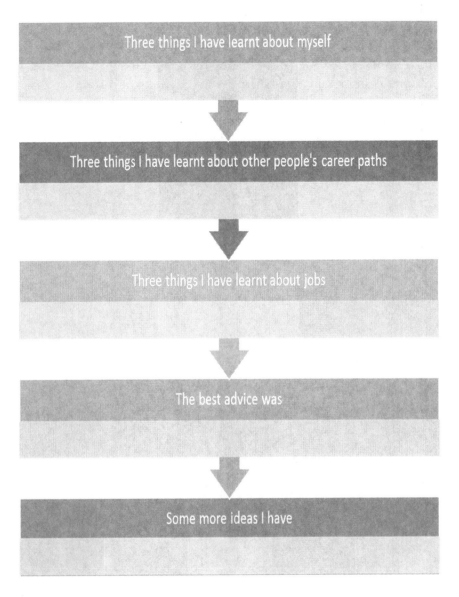

Review and support

To summarise so far, **Boot Camp** is about training. Although it requires commitment and effort to achieve things, it is so much easier with a mentor and support team. To make progress and be career fit, it requires analysing where you are at, finding out your priorities and making steps to achieve these goals. Don't be afraid to explore and try things out. But keep it real and achievable. Let your heart race with excitement and believe you can achieve your goals. Because you can.

Part 23

Making sure that you are going to get to the Showcase Final:

Knowledge about the opportunity

This is what the judges will be looking for so you have to do your research.

You will find a lot of information about this in the details about the vacancy/course. If it is an advertised vacancy, there will usually be a short description. It will identify the key features about the opportunity. This may include the job title, working hours and pay. Like an advert, it will highlight the key features of the opportunity. They are usually carefully put together and will mention the skills, experience and knowledge that they are looking for. Look at the words carefully - what are they describing? Enthusiastic? Committed? Keen? Experienced? Make a careful note as you will need to demonstrate how you match this.

There is likely to be a more detailed **job description** and **person specification** for the job. The **job description** gives details about the range of typical activities and duties that the post holder will be doing. It may also give an indication of the amount of time spent doing particular tasks or activities. The **person specification** is the crucial part of the application process as this is the main **marking criteria of the judges.** Just as the talent show judges know what to look out for, so the person specification lists in more detail the skills, experiences and knowledge that they want to see at application and at interview. They are likely to give clues about how important these skills, experiences and knowledge are by identifying whether they are essential (a must) or desirable (great if you have them but still apply if you don't).

If there is one thing that I can share with you it is that **this checklist will often give further clues about how they are assessed.** If it says 'application' next to certain items, it means that the judges will be looking for these things at the short listing stage when they look at all of the application forms. Short listing is when they decide on which people go through to the next stage for interview (the showcase finals). If it places 'interview' next to certain items on the checklist then you know that the judges will be specifically looking for evidence of these things at the interview stage. As a result, you can focus on these areas in your interview preparation.

They are looking for evidence from you and **more marks will be awarded if you can give them examples of how you have done this before and how it could be applied to this role.** We will spend more time on this in the **Showcase Final** section.

When it comes to applying to courses, entry requirements will be identified, including possible work experience placements. Prospectuses, web pages and the UCAS website will identify the requirements that are on the checklist. **It is your responsibility to look at all requirements and make sure that you can match them with your skills, knowledge and experience.**

Part 24

Making sure that you are going to get to the Showcase Final:

Knowledge about yourself

You need to know what you are good at and what you do well. You also need to know about the areas you need to work on. Doing this will give you knowledge about yourself. And having this knowledge will give you the confidence to impress the judges. It is all about knowing what rocks your world because when you know that you will be able to plan what you do next.

How can you prove it to the judges? **Knowledge about myself:**

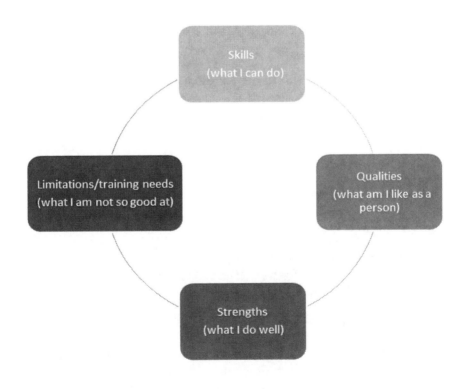

Part 25

Persuading the judges with an effective CV for employment

We have covered how a successful CV provides you with the opportunity to showcase your experiences and skills. If you haven't read those pages or not had to write a CV yet, you might want to refresh your memory about what makes a great CV (Part 7). Here we will focus very specifically on writing a CV for paid employment.

Start with name, address, phone number and email address. Include a website link if you have one.

Personal Profile

Explain your current situation. Make it clear if you have relevant qualifications and experience from the very outset.

Identify key words to 'sell' to the recruiter. Look at the words for the vacancy. This would also apply for a course. Don't copy directly from the website, but show that you are aware of what they are looking for.

Make it as specific as possible. Vague CVs at this point will look lazy.

Education and Qualifications

(Starting with the most recent first)

Where you studied (dates)

What you studied

Identify the things that will make them sit up and notice what you have to offer. Consider putting your A' levels or GCSEs in the order of priority (e.g. best grades or most relevant first). Explain briefly some courses that you have taken that they might not know, such as including assessed work experience or its equivalent.

Work Related Experience

Consider the order you put this in. Start with the most relevant to the opportunity. Remember that you are not just describing what you have done, but you are emphasising the key skills, knowledge and experience that you have gained that will be of interest and benefit to them. Avoid terms like 'I did...' but instead use active words, such as organised, researched, developed, responded, explained, supported, ensured, assisted, coordinated, delegated, managed, created...

Employment

Voluntary work

Business Related Activities

Additional skills and achievements

This is your chance to showcase additional skills such IT, languages spoken, driving licence, Sign Language or First Aid. Also include achievements from inside school and from a wider field such as sport or community and social groups. This may include positions of responsibility as well as prizes or nominations for awards or recognition. Employers/recruiters like to see what else you have achieved other than study.

Interests

It doesn't have to be too long a list, but it will give the reader an idea about what you like to do to unwind and spend your time. Avoid very general statements such as 'socialising with friends'. Be honest... they might ask you about it at interview or they could be an expert in it when you tried it only once five years ago...

References

It is usual to include two, one from education (school/college) and another from work experience, employment, part time job, voluntary work or group. Make sure that you have their permission first and check how they would prefer to be contacted.

Part 26

Same person, different jobs, two CVs

Imagine you have just left school with three A' levels and you are planning to apply for a job as a trainee Estate Agent. See how Sam could create a CV to identify the key skills and experiences that an Estate Agent may be interested in. By following the steps above, Sam looked at the opportunity first then looked at her own skills and experiences. She included all the information and emphasised the relevance to this particular role. Remember, if you want to see a CV which is formatted to two sides of A4 then take a look at the CV Examples page under VIP Access at www.whatrocksyourworld.com. Password **'wrywstar'**.

Sam Williams

35 Green Fields Way

Bramshall, Staffordshire

ST44 9OO

Samwilliams900@hotmail.co.uk

0144 900 900

Personal Profile

Accomplished A' level student with experience of business, the property sector and providing excellent customer service. Creative, numerate, confident and cooperative team member. Seeking training opportunities after A' levels to contribute towards the success within the property market.

Education and Qualifications

Bramshall High School, Bramshall   **2008 - 2013**

Jenny Mullins

A' levels Business Studies (A) Mathematics (B) IT (B)

A/S level General Studies (A)   2012

9 GCSEs   2011

All at grades A-C, including Maths (A) English Language (B) and Science (B,B)

Work Related Experience

Estate agency work experience

Haymans Estate Agents - Coltonvale (2 weeks)   **2011**

- Contributed to marketing team research of target properties within the area

- Assisted at presentation to operations manager

- Created spreadsheet of data and market value of properties for newsletter to 5,000 properties

Business Related Activities

Marketing manager, Young Enterprise - Bramshall High School   2010 - 2012

- Financial responsibility for budgeting and accurately maintaining balance sheets and bank account

- Produced accounts, business reports and updates to Young Enterprise management team

- Coordinated business launch and presented to business community audience

- Negotiated discounts and developed incentives for sale of product

- Developed marketing campaign though successful use of social media and viral marketing

Post it Printers and Marketing - Bramshall (2 week work experience)   2009

- Assisted the design team in creating customer leaflets using Mac design packages

- Created customer blog and "ask the team" enquiry page

Employment

Delivery and retail assistant - Dillons Newsagents, Bramshall   2009 - 2012

- Responsibility and initiative shown for managing money and balancing till

- Polite, friendly and respectful to customers across the community

- Organised to ensure orders delivered on time

Voluntary work

Fundraiser for Children in Need - Bramshall High School   Nov 2010

- Financial responsibility from collecting donations, checking money raised and ensuring payment is made

- Encouraging participation in fund-raising activities from cake baking through to fancy dress

- Effective teamwork with both students and teachers

Additional skills and achievements

Year 11 class rep and awarded merit for school community award

Nominated to represent school at Regional Young Enterprise competition

Conversational French and Spanish

British Sign Language (level A)

Fully competent in practical application of range of IT packages, including Mac, Microsoft Word, Excel, PowerPoint.

Interests

Social Media design, cross country running and charity fundraising

References

Mr Kenneth	Mrs Dillon
Bramshall High School	Dillons News Agent
Windy End	1, The Square
Bramshall	Bramshall
ST44 1AA	ST44 1BB

Question: If Sam was going to apply for a training position in online marketing, how might she change her CV?

Sam Williams

35 Green Fields Way

Bramshall, Staffordshire

ST44 9OO

Samwilliams900@hotmail.co.uk

0144 900 900

Personal Profile

Accomplished A' level student with experience of creative design and marketing. Creative, numerate, confident and cooperative team member.

Seeking training opportunities after A' levels to contribute as part of a vibrant marketing company.

Education and Qualifications

Bramshall High School, Bramshall   **2008 - 2013**

A' levels Business Studies (A) Mathematics (B) IT (B)

A/S level General Studies (A)   2012

9 GCSEs, all at grades A-C, including Maths (A) English Language (B) and Science
(B,B)   2011

Fully competent in practical application of range of IT packages, including Mac, Microsoft Word, Excel, PowerPoint.

Work Related Experience

Marketing and Business Related Activities

Marketing manager, Young Enterprise - Bramshall High School   2010 - 2012

- Coordinated business launch and presented to business community audience

- Developed marketing campaign though successful use of social media and viral marketing

- Negotiated discounts and developed incentives for sale of product

- Financial responsibility for budgeting and accurately maintaining balance sheets and bank accounts

- Produced accounts, business reports and updates to Young Enterprise management team

Post it Printers and Marketing - Bramshall (2 week work experience)   2009

- Assisted the design team in creating customer leaflets using Mac design packages

- Created customer blog and "ask the team" enquiry page

Estate agency work experience

Haymans Estate Agents - Coltonvale (2 weeks)   2011

- Contributed to marketing team research of target properties within the area

- Assisted at presentation to operations manager

- Created spreadsheet of data and market value of properties for newsletter to 5,000 properties

Employment

Delivery and retail assistant - Dillons Newsagents, Bramshall   2009-2012

- Responsibility and initiative shown for managing money and balancing till

- Polite, friendly and respectful to customers across the community

- Organised to ensure orders delivered on time

Voluntary work

Fundraiser for Children in Need - Bramshall High School   Nov 2010

- Financial responsibility from collecting donations, checking money raised and ensuring payment is made

- Encouraging participation in fund raising activities from cake baking through to fancy dress

- Effective teamwork with both students and teachers

Additional skills and achievements

Year 11 class rep and awarded merit for school community award

Nominated to represent school at Regional Young Enterprise competition

Conversational French and Spanish

British Sign Language (level A)

Interests

Social Media design, cross country running and charity fundraising

References

Mr Kenneth	Mrs Dillon
Bramshall High School	Dillons News Agent
Windy End	1, The Square
Bramshall	Bramshall
ST44 1AA	ST44 1BB

Spot the differences? It comes back to knowing what your 'judge' is looking for and making it clear what you have and what you can do to shine in this role.

Part 27

Same person, one advertised job and one speculative enquiry, two covering letters

This applies to both the CV and the covering letter. If it is responding to a vacancy, make sure that in the first paragraph you refer to where you saw the opportunity advertised and include the reference number. Be as specific as you can so they know that you have done your research.

It could therefore look something like this:

Samantha Williams

35 Green Fields Way

Bramshall, Staffordshire

ST44 9OO

Tel. 0144 900 900

Samwilliams900@hotmail.co.uk

Ms Lucy Griffiths

Ward Property Services

Old Newton Way

Bramshall

ST45 1QQ

August 23rd 2013

Dear Ms Griffiths,

In response to your job advert for trainee sales negotiator, as advertised in '*The Post*' 18th August 2013, please find enclosed a copy of my CV, detailing my skills and experiences as requested.

Having gained previous work experience in the estate agency sector, I would be keen to join the team at Ward Property Services in Bramshall. As a resident of Bramshall, I am aware of the success of Ward providing effective customer service to its clients in both the residential and commercial sector. As an established business I know that I would be working with a committed team who have successfully maintained business during the recession. The training scheme leading to a recognised qualification appeals to me as I know that I thrive on working hard and can achieve at a high level.

My previous work experience and part time jobs have enabled me to gain excellent experience in the residential property sector, from dealing with clients and contributing to marketing campaigns. In addition I gained positions of responsibility as the treasurer and marketing manager for a Young Enterprise project. The challenge of working to create a successful business and work with others had motivated me to do the best that I can. My A' levels taught me not only the understanding of how businesses work, but also the numerical and computing skills needed to succeed. Recently I was nominated for my role in Young Enterprise at a regional level. I believe in putting others first in what I do and creating a good team environment.

I look forward to a career in property management and am committed to making the most of the training opportunities on offer. Thank you for taking the time to read my letter of application and CV and I look forward to hearing from you soon.

Yours sincerely,

Samantha Williams

But what if you haven't seen the opportunity you want advertised at all? Then be proactive and get speculative! Just because the opportunity isn't advertised doesn't mean that it doesn't exist. Think back to the **Audition Stage** when you interviewed people about their career paths. I am sure you will have talked to people who 'found' their opportunity by being in the right place at the right time, or by asking their network and making enquiries. You may well have found your own part time job or work experience from contacting people to find out if they had any opportunities or would be prepared to offer you an opportunity. With speculative applications you have to make sure that you get that first impression absolutely right. Do all the preparation beforehand and make sure that you have got your facts right. That means checking for names, addresses and contact details and making sure that you have got the spelling absolutely right. Use Google or yell.com to be sure.

With the previous covering letter, the first paragraph:

"In response to your job advert for trainee sales negotiator, as advertised in 'The Post' 18th August 2013, please find enclosed a copy of my CV, detailing my skills and experiences as requested,"

Could be pitched as:

"to enquire about the possibility of any job vacancies in... or opportunities within your company (add name of organisation)"

Make it clear whether it is just a job or whether you would be keen to take advantage of work experience/shadowing.

With the second paragraph demonstrate what you know about the company and the roles within it. Make it personal to them. Your next paragraph shows that you have matched your skills and experience to the company and the roles that they have. Focus on your commitment to making the most of any opportunities and your willingness to learn from experts in that sector.

Do thank them for taking the time and stress your availability to discuss further.

Part 28

Persuading the judges with an effective application form

Whether it's an online application or in paper format you need to be clear on what the judges will be looking for so you have to do your research.

Look at this example:

Job vacancy

Trainee Online Marketing Person required for growing marketing company, Click Biz. Know your pokes from your tweets? As we expand into social media, we require a creative and dynamic person to work with our clients to target the under 25 market. You will have good communication skills, have great ideas and understand how the market works. Ideally you will be educated to A' level standard and be keen to progress in the marketing business.

Essential Qualifications:

Good standard of education to include:

GCSEs grades B including English Language and Maths

Knowledge:

Knowledge of major social media platforms

Experience:

School/college based work experience

Skills:

Good communication skills

Team worker

Desirable Qualifications

A' levels

Studied Business/Design

Knowledge:

Prezi and SurveyMonkey

Experience:

Experience in marketing and design

Skills:

Apple Mac

Qualities:

Creative

Dynamic

Innovative

Start with the checklist:

To make this application stand out start off by identifying what they are looking for in the advert and highlight these areas...

Job vacancy

Trainee Online Marketing Person required for **growing** marketing company, **Click Biz. Know** your pokes from your tweets? As we expand **into social media**, we require a **creative** and **dynamic** person to work with our **clients** to **target the under 25 market.** You will have **good communication skills**, have **great ideas** and **understand how the market works.** Ideally you will be educated to A' level standard and be **keen to progress** in the marketing business.

Make sure that you have the essential qualifications that they are looking for:

Essential Qualifications:

Good standard of education to include

GCSEs grades B including English Language and Maths

Do you have the desirable qualifications?

Desirable Qualifications:

A' levels

Studied Business/Design

Essential Knowledge:

Knowledge of major social media platforms

Now identify the knowledge that you have. What do you know and how have you applied it in the past? Give examples of your use and the range of your knowledge.

Throughout my studies and work experience I have developed a personal website, linked to my Twitter and LinkedIn profile. As part of my marketing role in Young Enterprise I developed a marketing strategy, including tweeting updates and viral marketing.

Desirable Knowledge:

Prezi and SurveyMonkey

If you've got this, make a big deal about it. They are seeing this as huge bonus. Again, identify examples of how you have used it, your involvement and the range of applications. They will be excited if you have this!

Designing surveys by using SurveyMonkey enhanced our feedback analysis in my Young Enterprise company. Creating questions that were relevant to our client group meant I could present findings to the management team and simplify our key findings. In addition, I taught myself how to use Prezi via an online course after I saw it showcased on my work experience placement and used it as part of my A' level course work.

Continue with the checklist and jot down some examples of how you can meet this checklist under the headings. Don't forget, that if it says that it is essential you must make sure that it is included in your application form. Check that you have covered everything on the checklist.

Experience:

School/college based work experience

Experience in marketing and design

Outline the experiences that you have gained, identifying what was part of your studies, as well as the experience that you have arranged yourself. This can show initiative and commitment. Focus on the benefits of experience gained and show it can be relevant to the company Click Biz.

Continue with the skills section and then prioritise the examples that you have and decide which will have the most impact. Ideally you don't want to write more than two pages of A4.

Structure your points in the order that they are listed in the person specification. For example, knowledge and qualifications first, then relevant experience, then skills and qualities. This will make it easier for the judges to put ticks on their own checklist. You really want to get on their right side as quickly as possible.

When you have done this you'll write the opening paragraph so it needs to grab their attention for all the right reasons. Don't be afraid to let them know how much you want this opportunity. Make it very specific so that they know that you have taken the time to pitch it **just to Click Biz.** Show that you have done your research. Let them know why you want this job, what stood out for you and why you believe that you meet and exceed their expectations.

Part 29

See if you can answer these questions:

My greatest achievement was:
The thing that 'rocked my world' during my placement was:
What makes me stand out from the crowd is:
The list of skills, achievements and experiences I can include in my CV and applications:

With an application form, there will be sections that require you to complete all of your personal details, such as name and contact information as well as qualifications taken and place of study. There may be sections on additional training and qualifications, as well as any work experience or employment. Aim to be accurate and honest. If you are offered the job or place on a course based on this information and you cannot provide evidence of this then you may have your offer withdrawn. Getting a place under false pretences would be considered fraud.

Ask a friend, family member or mentor if they would be happy to read through your application and check that you have completed all sections and that all spelling and grammar is correct.

It is the section at the end of the application form that will enable you to really demonstrate to the recruiter that you have done your research and have what it takes to be successful in this opportunity. Whether it is called additional or supporting information, or even a personal statement, the purpose is for you to demonstrate why you are interested in this opportunity and what you have to offer.

To make this application stand out:

Start off by identifying what they are looking for and write these areas down. Please look at the previous section to get an idea of the right sequence you should use.

Everything will be under headings such as 'qualifications', 'skills', 'experience', 'knowledge' and 'qualities'.

Jot down some examples of how you can meet this checklist under these headings... don't forget, that if it says that it is essential then you must make sure that it is included in your application form.

Check that you have covered everything on the checklist.

Prioritise the examples that you have and decide which will have the most impact. Ideally you don't want to write more than two pages of A4. Many application forms will have a strict word limit. Some online applications will even specify the number of characters and lines available.

Then, imagine that you have just 20 seconds to impress the judge and show them your passion and interests in this opportunity. What would you say? This is going to be your opening paragraph so it needs to grab their attention for all the right reasons. Don't be afraid to let them know how much you want this opportunity. Make it very specific so that they know that you have taken the time to pitch it just to them.

Start to structure your points together in paragraph form, with each section focussing on the key criteria. Read it out loud to hear how it sounds. If it sounds like a shopping list of 'I...this' and 'I...that', you will send the reader to sleep!

Focus on the positives and remove any references that say 'only', 'couldn't' etc. Don't undersell yourself or give them any reason to believe you can't do it. Instead focus on positive words. Avoid telling your entire life story and going into elaborate and unnecessary details. Instead focus on the relevant experiences and skills they are looking for.

Go through the draft again. Have you shown that you have done your research about the opportunity? Met all of the criteria for that job or course? Given strong examples? Written with enthusiasm?

Piece all of the paragraphs together and read it out loud again. Are you convincing? Are you enthusiastic? Are you positive? Do the judges want to see you in person?

You need your enthusiasm to shine out... after all you know the competition and you want to take your place at the finals, so they can 'judge' you and meet you in person.

Boot Camp has been hard and as you've realised, there's no room for shortcuts or quick fixes. The shortlisted finalists are about to be announced and you've made it.

But, what if you haven't made it straightaway? Don't give up! I truly believe that there will be many opportunities for you to get to the finals. But if you need some encouragement, then read on.

Part 30

When it doesn't appear to be going to plan

It is natural to have doubts and not even the best laid plans necessarily go the way that we had hoped. Something that helps me to put things into perspective and to encourage me, is this wise saying, which is on my notice board at work. It's called the Serenity Challenge (from the excellent book *'The Happiness Trap'* by Dr Russ Harris).

"Develop the courage to solve the problems that can be solved, the serenity to accept those problems that cannot be solved and the wisdom to know the difference."

What I can do is: **solve the problems that can be solved.** I can control how well I prepare for an application/interview by researching about the opportunity. I can find out what it is about, the organisation as well as the career area in general. By giving time to preparation, my CVs and applications will not be rushed and will present me in the best light. If I don't know where to start, I can talk to my mentor and support network. I may need to go back to some of the earlier exercises and review my targets. I am not on my own and there are people who can guide me and support me, but I may need to listen more, be honest about where I am at and make sure that I do my best.

Serenity or peace about the problems that cannot be solved. We are all part of a much bigger picture and although we are all unique and talented, we may not be able to influence everything. If a College or University has just 50 places on its course, we cannot change that. If they have decided to use assessment tests or set certain grade requirements, we cannot change that. Deadline is 15th October? Then we have to meet the deadline or risk not being interviewed. A recession hits and job losses made. As individuals we cannot reverse a global economy overnight.

What we **can do** is to focus our energies on what we can change or solve. Wisdom comes from knowing which battles to fight or which problems we can solve or change. The problem with some talent shows, indeed the celebrity culture, is that it can look like overnight success. For a very small minority this might be the case. When 'stars' are discovered they have usually spent years trying to get their big break or be recognised, including years in training or in boot camp. They have had their own doubts along the way, faced criticism, setbacks or exhaustion. There are plenty of inspirational stories that you can read to encourage you to have the strength and courage to solve your own problems. Read the stories from Olympic gold medallist Jessica Ennis and about how she overcame injuries. Or Bradley Wiggins and his years of training to win the Tour de France as well as Olympic golds. Then there's Bear Grylls – he has survived some of the world's toughest terrains or challenges. Finally, there's Michelle Obama's visit to the school, with her inspirational speech to her teenage audience, recorded on YouTube.

If you were writing your own life story, you'd see that through challenges you have had the opportunity to make decisions. Some good and possibly some bad, but hopefully you have learnt from them. I like to try and keep these events into perspective and play the *'Friends'* theme tune and give them imaginary titles, such as, *The one where Jenny forgot the deadline'* or *The one where the interviewer didn't find Jenny's answers convincing.'*

Don't let your dreams get stolen. Instead surround yourself with positive people, such as your mentor. Remind yourself about the people you interviewed at the **Audition Stage** and the career paths that people take. A lot of people may not have got everything they ever wanted straightaway but I bet when they got their prize, it felt great.

Keep on keeping on and if it feels hard on your own gather your support team around you.

What's stopping you?

Tweet Challenge: What is the main thing you have learnt about yourself in this section? How would you persuade the judges to invite you to the showcase finals? Need some encouragement? Tweet me @whatrocksyou.

SHOWCASE FINAL

In this final section, it is time to let the hard work pay off and for your talent to shine. Let's show that you have done your research and can demonstrate how you stand out from the crowd. We will look at discovering what is on the judges' checklist and how to survive being under the spotlight. By demonstrating your own experience and style, we can put that talent to work and shine when it really matters.

So, you've made it! From the very first ideas, to trying it out and getting the best out of your mentors/supporters, the **Showcase Final** has arrived. The finals seemed such a long time away from the auditions but now the judges are in their seats and waiting. It's your opportunity to show that you have done your training and prove that the preparation and experience has paid off. Getting to that interview is almost the end of this journey.

But we've still got some way to go. Because we've got competition. And **they** are keen to impress the judges too. Let's focus on what will make you stand out.

By now, you should have lots of information about yourself. You should know what you are good at from the following areas: subjects taken, skills developed from work experience, voluntary work, business related activities, sports, interests and achievements. You have had feedback from mentors, coaches, teachers, employers and people from work experience. You will have created a CV for a specific purpose in mind, such as work experience or a job. And if they are advertising for a CV, you will need to pitch it **exactly to their requirements**. It isn't enough to use exactly the same CV for every opportunity. The same is true for application forms. When it comes to the additional/supporting information section, you will need to write a new one and pitch it **exactly to their requirements**.

We are now moving it up a notch. Your dream opportunity is in front of you. It could be a full time job or a place on a course. And you have the best news ever - they want to meet you. The spotlight has been switched on and it is inching its way towards you...

When it comes to being centre stage at an interview, all the hard work has taken place beforehand. Clearly the application worked. All those lessons learnt from your mentor, all of the targets on your training plan, the CVs written, the research, the visits. It's got you to the short list. Of the many applications (and it could be thousands) they want to see **you**.

The **Showcase Final** is all about the three Ps:

Preparation

Presentation

Positivity

Preparation

Just Me, **Audition Stage** and **Boot Camp** focussed on preparation. It has required so much hard work and support. The time has come to show how it will pay off. But getting in front of those judges for the first time, what will it feel like? What will it look like?

How do you really know what's on the judges' checklist? The questions that they are likely to ask are to find out if you meet their requirements. The clues that they have given to the list can be found by doing some preparation and research. Just as we needed to know the checklist when we made our initial applications, we need to go back to this list for the interviews at the showcase finals.

Their items on **their** checklist can be found in:

Job/course details

Prospectus

The website of the organisation

Person specification

Open day visits

Forums

Work experience/shadowing

But **Showcase Final** is a two way process. The judges need to know about you and see how you not only meet their criteria, but how you exceed it.

My Checklist: About M E - 'Meet and Exceed'

Whether it is for a course, job or placement this is how I can demonstrate that I **meet** and **exceed** their criteria.

My Checklist: About M E 'meet and exceed'

Whether it is for a course, job or placement this is how I can demonstrate that I **meet** and **exceed** their criteria:

1) Highlight the key words from these areas:

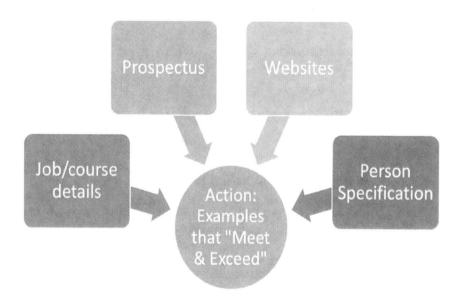

2) Find examples that demonstrate how you meet and exceed.

3) Identify what you have learnt about **them** and **yourself**.

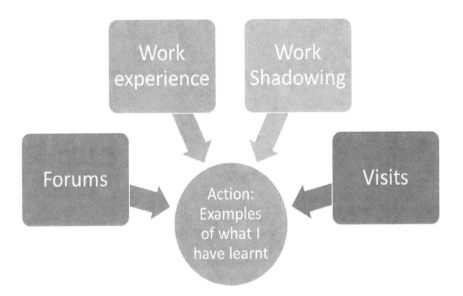

4) Provide examples of what you have learnt.

From these activities you should have plenty of examples that show how you meet and exceed and what you have learnt. To be successful, start off with your findings under the following headings.

Why **them:** role, course, organisation. How this links in to your bigger goals. Show that you have taken the time to find out about them. This will show your interest and enthusiasm.

Your experience:	• How it is relevant to this role. • Go back to your education/studies, work experience, part time jobs, extra curricular activities, hobbies and interests.
Your knowledge:	• Specific information you have learnt from subjects, courses and talking to people.
Your skills:	• Specific things that you can do, such as communication, team work, problem solving, time management, organisation, IT, research and laboratory skills.
Your qualities:	• What you are like as a person and how you can be described. • Look at feedback from mentors, friends, family, teachers, work experience placement, youth leaders, sports team and voluntary work.

Arrange a dress rehearsal

A great way to prepare is to practise beforehand with your mentor and rehearse as though it was real. To make it as authentic as possible give them as much information about the opportunity beforehand including the job/course requirements and the process of **Showcase Final**. To help them, identify six areas that you know are on the judges' checklist. They may also want to add a score to each question, so that you can be given a mark.

Here are some questions that you might want to give them to help them prepare. Their role is to be as constructive as possible. Ideally they should run through the questions as though it was for real and give you some feedback afterwards.

Why are you interested in this role?

What attracted you to…?

Tell me about your relevant experience.

How have your studies/experience helped to prepare you for this role?

What skills have you gained that will make you successful?

Tell me about a time when you had to... lead a team... overcome a challenge... respond to criticism... work towards a goal...?

What have you done to prepare for this interview... this role?

What are your strengths and weaknesses?

Describe yourself in twenty seconds/three words?

What are your career goals/plans?

Where would you like to be in one, three, five, ten years' time?

Areas they should concentrate on are:

How well you answered the questions: did you 'meet and exceed'?

Clarity (such as any hesitation, incomplete answers?)

How you came across, including evidence of enthusiasm and motivation. Are there any fidgets, mannerisms, lack of eye contact?

After the feedback, jot down what you have learnt about the experience and what you have learnt about yourself.

Make it SMART

Next time, I will prepare by focusing on:

Good tips my mentor shared with me:

Preparation: the day itself

"By failing to prepare you are preparing to fail."

Benjamin Franklin

There are a number of key preparations that you need to make to ensure that you are ready for the day that you meet the judges. When it comes to getting to the venue, work out how you are going to get there and build in extra time to allow for delays, as well as finding parking spaces. Make sure that you have the exact location. The interview may be in a different place to where you have been before. To avoid panicking about being late, put the contact details in your phone as soon as possible, so you can at least let them know that you are likely to be late. Once they know they are likely to be able to re-arrange or at least advise you about where to go.

If you are travelling on your own, make sure that you have some key items with you.

Money: take enough to cover an emergency change in plan, such as for a taxi or parking meter.

Phone: put the contact details you have been given in your phone but make sure that it is switched off or on silent before going into the building. You really don't want it to ring or vibrate during that key moment. There's a very good chance that you will have blown your opportunity if you have left it on.

Documentation/portfolio: check to see if you are expected to take any documentation with you. This could be a birth certificate or personal ID. It may also include exam certificates, references or even sample coursework. To give a professional and positive impression, consider buying a folder or portfolio to keep all your documentation in. One with clear plastic pockets works best. But make sure you know where everything is - you don't want it to look as though you are disorganised and don't know where things are.

Water and tissue: especially if you have a cold or hay fever.

Presenting yourself: first impressions

Unless specifically told what they expect you to wear you should dress smartly. This also means clean clothes and shoes. First impressions really do matter and judges will form a very quick impression of you by what you are wearing and how you come across. Generally speaking most interviewers will be looking for you to show that you have taken the time to get ready and get your first impression right.

Avoid anything that might distract the judges. This can include: excessive jewellery, badges or clothes with slogans or big logos. Avoid garish colours if you are applying for a more traditional opportunity. Trainers, flip flops or incredibly high heels can be great in other environments but are best avoided at interviews.

If possible, avoid smoking and drinking or eating where it can leave an after taste/smell. Think of a time when you are in a confined space and someone's got an overpowering smell. By all means take a mint beforehand, but never ever chew gum. Perfume and body spray should be discreet.

When it comes to your outfit, here's a top tip to see if it is appropriate: sit down in front of a full-length mirror. This will usually give you an idea if it is too tight/short or revealing. Can you move your arms around? I once saw someone wearing a shirt which was so tight that he couldn't move his arms in a presentation! This was entertaining for me but highly embarrassing for the candidate. So although you can get to centre stage, bear in mind the interview room might be so small you can barely move.

Be minimalistic in what you take along: required items are your portfolio, documentation and memory stick. I remember once interviewing someone who had been shopping beforehand so brought that along too! Not a great first impression.

Presentation

To think about first impressions, I'd like you to do some research. Switch on your TV, preferably a programme where you won't recognise any of the people. Turn the sound off and watch the people interacting. This can also work well if it's a film in a foreign language. Study what they look like and jot down your first impressions. Observe how they communicate. You won't know what they are saying but can you work out their mood or temperament? Happy? Sad? Excited? Angry? Turn the sound on and listen if you can detect any clues or information. You might notice accents, whether they speak quietly or show enthusiasm.

Surprised that you have learnt so much simply by watching people? Look at the list of things that you noticed. Of course, it isn't the whole picture, but as human beings we are quite savvy at observing people and forming impressions. After a while we might change our opinion, but first impressions are powerful and that impact may take some time to change.

A number of studies have focussed on how we communicate and what we notice. One study by Mehrabian uses an equation that:

Communication is…

55% non-verbal communication (body language and posture)

38% voice tone, variety, pitch and variation

With just 7% spoken words

Although others have suggested slightly different percentages, the point remains that our body gives clues to what we are feeling or thinking.

What does this mean for the **Showcase Final?**

It means that even before you say a word your non-verbal communication is giving clues and signals. This might be how you are feeling, such as confidence level, enthusiasm and commitment.

To give a good positive first impression, here are some tips to help you appear more confident, interested and in control (even if you do feel sick with nerves and desperate to escape the spotlight).

Eye contact and gaze. It has been said that our eyes are the window to our souls. In other words, our eyes can give away so much about our interests and emotions. Eye contact can indicate how interested we are and where we are engaged. Ever heard a teacher criticise a student for not listening, because they were looking out of the window? Now they might actually be listening, but because they looked away it gave the impression of being distracted or not interested. Much research has gone into our eye direction and how this can relate to our thoughts and memories.

Here are a few exercises that you could try with a friend or by looking in the mirror. Best not try it on random strangers!

Stare for 5-10 seconds without blinking. When did it feel uncomfortable?

Open eyes wider when explaining an idea. Did it convey interest?

Look away every time someone talks to you. What response did you get?

Facial Expressions: this can include smiling/frowning. My mum always reminded me that it took fewer muscles and less energy to smile than to frown. It really doesn't matter where you are in the world - a smile is understood in any language. Although there might be some cultural differences about eye contact and gaze, with a friendly smile you convey that you are happy to be there and engage.

Posture and gestures: how you 'hold yourself' is also important in creating a positive impression and that you are keen to interact. It includes how you sit and stand and move your body (such as slouch or lean). It can also be called 'building rapport', where you show to someone that you are actively listening and engaging in the process. Holding your shoulders back not only makes you look more confident but you are also allowing more air to get into your lungs. As you breathe more deeply, you relax and control nerves better. When seated avoid crossing arms, legs and clutching your stomach. It looks as though you are uncomfortable and could give the impression that you don't want to be there, or even that you are holding things back. Using your hands can help to explain a point, but avoid fidgeting.

Contact: this refers to 'touches' related to communication, such as a handshake, pat on the back or even kissing. The meaning depends on the situation and it's important to work out the right environment. For the Showcase Final, the way to greet people would be to make a firm handshake, make eye contact and smile.

Distance: while we might like our family and friends to stand close to us, it is a good idea in public to observe a distance where we don't invade personal body space. If you are meeting people for the first time make sure that you don't make them feel too uncomfortable. Leave a little space between you and them.

Shine bright like a diamond

Understanding how we come across can help us create a positive first impression as well as ensure that we don't give out the wrong message. From the moment you arrive to the moment you leave, you are being watched. The **Showcase Final** begins when you enter the building and meet the receptionist. It ends when you leave that building. Therefore create a positive impression with everyone you meet. See the whole day as the culmination of your hard work.

When the spotlight is on, how do you know that you are doing well and impressing those judges? The great thing about communication is that it is two way. When you are sending out messages, so are they. If you are introduced to anyone, politely offer your hand, smile and make eye contact. Chances are they will do the same. You are nearly there! After a brief introduction, they will start with their questions. If you are being asked to deliver a presentation, they will often do this first. The final has truly begun.

Being positive and focusing on success

Remember, you have prepared, had a dress rehearsal with your mentor and looked at how to present yourself. You have de-coded non-verbal communication and now it's time to look at what to say and how to say it.

Three words to help you remember success in the showcase finals:

GOLD: Go On Let's Deliver

SHINE: Show How I Naturally Excel

STAR: Situation Task Action Result

Going for GOLD: Go On Let's Deliver focuses on mentally preparing for the final and looking at how important our body language and presentation is. It's about believing that you can do it! You can engage in a positive way and show that you have put in lots of hard work for that moment when it really matters. Plus, you want to make sure that you know what's on their checklist and prove it. Nerves are a natural response to the environment but can be controlled by deep breathing and making sure that you know your stuff. Putting yourself in the zone is about being focussed and maintaining control of what you can control. Walk tall and enter the stage.

Go for GOLD: Go On Let's Deliver

You can use this to your advantage. If the judges are nodding and smiling, it's likely to be going well as they are engaged and listening. They may even be mirroring your own body language which often happens when rapport exists and they are comfortable with the process. Are they focussing on your eyes, appearing engaged and actively listening? But what happens if you think they are bored or not impressed? Or if they appear distracted or they are not listening? After all you might be the eighth person that they have seen in a day.

All is not lost and you can regain control. Focus on their eyes and smile. Consider moving forward slightly and encouraging them to listen. Use your tone and pitch to convey enthusiasm and show how interested you are. Make sure that you are giving them plenty of positive examples to keep them engaged. If there are a number of judges who are busy writing things down, ensure that you include all of your judges. This can be achieved by simply glancing across to all of the judges. Don't just focus your answer to the judge that asked you the question. You need to include them all. After all, the judges will all need to agree and reach a consensus that you are going to be awarded the opportunity.

SHINE: Show How I Naturally Excel

This looks at what you say: the examples, your strengths and the lessons that you have learnt. We have looked at them earlier under your Experience, Knowledge, Skills and Qualities. It's easy to respond to questions by producing information or facts. But to truly shine you need to convey enthusiasm and show that you exceed their expectations. Good ways that you can do this are to use positive and action focussed language. We looked at this in **Boot Camp** with CVs and applications, but the same rules apply. Focus on the positives and what you did that will be of interest to them. Identify your contribution and the successes. Again, avoid language such as 'only', 'hardly', and 'rarely'.

The message needs to be that you can apply what you have learnt to other situations that will be of interest to the judges. In other words, focus on your potential and the benefits that you can bring. Excelling and exceeding means going further than everyone else and making it your intention to strive to do your best. Even if you haven't had any direct experience, talk about **how** you would approach a situation. Allow the judges to see that you have determination to succeed and have used your time in school/college/work experience to find out more. Being committed to your own future will demonstrate to the judges that you have been working towards this moment with careful preparation. Let them see that your support network has helped you to get to this point but that this **Showcase Final** has always been your end goal and the target that you have been working towards.

The judges are ultimately looking to see if you have drive, commitment and the willingness to be part of a team. They are not necessarily looking for the finished product, but they need to be confident that you are presenting the combination of exact ingredients that they can work with. The whole process of recruiting is costly and time consuming. The judges (and entire production team) have invested so much in getting their checklist together that they need to know that they are making the right decisions.

STAR: Situation Task Action Result

Finally, the judges are poised over the marks for each question. From the very beginning of this process I have encouraged you to keep a record of your ideas and plans. Targets have been specific and I have encouraged you to keep a reminder of your achievements. The time has come for you to use your audience time with the judges to make these examples come alive. STAR is a great structure to help you emphasise the key points of your examples and to hold their attention.

Imagine that the judges ask for an example of when you worked as part of a team. The temptation is to give them lots of description such as identities, names, time of day, month, year, places and locations. But this isn't a story. It is your golden opportunity to give an example that will meet and exceed their criteria. It is also designed to influence and show that you have skills that can be transferred to another situation.

Apply STAR to your example:

Situation and Task should take up 30% of your answer. Briefly describe the context. For example:

In year 12, I co-ordinated the market research as part of a team of six members in Young Enterprise.

Follow this with 70% of your answer describing the Action and Result. This is where you get your marks as they will be focussing on how you approach tasks, the skills that you used, what they can learn about you as a person and how that affected the final result.

Draw out what you have learnt and focus on your personal contribution. For example:

During this time, I researched the market by using a SurveyMonkey that I had created. Throughout the process, I kept everyone informed via Facebook and emails and arranged for regular updates. When I collated the results, I presented the findings to the team and explained what I had discovered. Responding to their questions, we developed an action plan to launch the product. After this process, we reviewed our progress together at our team meetings. This year we sold over 500 branded water bottles across the community.

At the end of the day, all of the judges will meet together and compare notes. By giving them examples (using STAR) they will be able to identify the things that they are looking for and compare your examples with other people's comments. This is why we have spent so much time establishing examples and evidence that will persuade the judges of your commitment and achievements.

What's your style?

What makes you different? What makes you stand out? What will make the hairs stand up on the back of their necks? What will give them goose bumps? The answer - putting your talent to work.

So how do you get the judges out of their seats? That comes down to your own X factor. In other words that magic ingredient that they are looking for. And because it's your X factor it's hard to describe. But spend time looking at the people you admire who are successful. It could have been the people that have supported you from those early stages. It could be the advice and tips they have given you. It could have been someone you admired from your work experience. Whatever makes them stand out, see if you can emulate this. The hard work has all gone on behind the scenes. You have needed commitment to succeed even when you have had doubts or couldn't see the next step. It is about letting the judges know that you are actively taking control of your life and that you want to win. They will see your passion and your hard work by your preparation from work experience, effective applications and the interview itself.

You need them to make a unanimous decision and appoint you.

So, they have asked their questions. They've gained an impression about you from what you have said and how you have presented yourself. You may have been asked to talk them through your portfolio. But this isn't an interrogation. Because you have prepared for this moment - and it shows.

Just before you are asked to exit the centre stage the judges will usually give you the opportunity to ask them questions. Even though every ounce of you is desperate to head off stage, just pause a moment. Ask them some questions. Not personal ones, but ones that demonstrate that you have done your homework on the role and opportunity. Ask how long it will be before you find out. What training is offered? What support is available for new people? Are there mentors available? Your questions will be giving positive signals that you are keen to progress with this organisation or course. You have goals and passion. But avoid questions about salary (wait till it's offered) or information that is easily found out on websites.

And like any showcase final, when the winner is announced, it's your team of supporters that you want to thank. Remember they believed in you. So take an imaginary bow and enjoy your success.

POSTSCRIPT

But what happens if doesn't work first time round and you were a runner up?

So, you got a round of applause and you scored well. But you missed out. Gutted.

It's okay to feel gutted. Really, it's okay. But (and here it comes), try and see it as excellent experience and learn from the process. As with the dress rehearsal, sit down and go back through the questions and ask yourself how you thought that you did and how you could improve for next time. Make notes that you can refer to when you next meet with your mentor and prepare for the next opportunity. You may also be given the chance to ask for feedback from the judges/interviewers. Although you may be very disappointed, do thank them for their time and the opportunity to be interviewed. Nobody likes a sore loser, so even though it might not be that comfortable, listen to their comments and advice. Their feedback is likely to be constructive and helpful. Give yourself time to take on board what they are saying. You may not agree with them at this point, but don't use this as an opportunity to lash back, even if it's tempting. Think of all the people who storm off at the talent shows when they are given difficult feedback... never pretty and awkward for all concerned.

With the feedback, identify areas that you can work on or change. Your mentor will be able to help you with action points here. In my experience as an interviewer, most people can improve by taking their time and giving examples that demonstrate the required skills and knowledge. If you found that nerves got the better of you, go back to the relaxation techniques mentioned earlier on in this chapter. You are still a contender.

But please don't give up! Whether it's the individual stories of Olympic champions, discoveries by scientists, intrepid explorers or inventors, the message is that success came after much training, trials, setbacks and experiments. Very few people are overnight successes. Get back into the competition, brush yourself off and be proactive and find your next opportunity. Believe that you have what it takes and go for it! Continue to be inspired by the stories of Olympic medallists: find them on YouTube.

Need more experience? Go get it! Need another dress rehearsal? Go to your mentor to practise again. Need new action points? Work at them and use your support network.

YOU CAN DO IT!

Tweet Challenge: Tell me what you think of this book. Tweet me @whatrocksyou.

ABOUT THE AUTHOR

Jenny Mullins is a Careers Adviser with over 20 years' experience working with young people. Her passion is to help young people work out what they want to do with their lives and support them to achieve their goal. She has worked across the country in schools, colleges, youth groups and universities. She works at the University of Birmingham, UK. Enthusiastic and committed to raising aspirations, she was awarded a National Careers Award in 2008. Known amongst her friends for having a very silly sense of humour as well as possibly the world's loudest sneezes, she often tells people that she keeps bees (she doesn't keep bees but it always gets a reaction). She would like to travel more, loves the Adrian Mole diaries and hopes to write more books in the future. Say hi to Jenny at www.whatrocksyourworld.com or follow her on Twitter @whatrocksyou.

CPSIA information can be obtained at www.ICGtesting.com
Printed in the USA
LVOW12s1559090514

385159LV00017B/1039/P